H.S. VIGEVENO

IN THE EYE

OF THE

AP<u>O</u>CALYPSE

H.S. VIGEVENO

IN THE EYE
OF THE
AP<u>O</u>CALYPSE

UNDERSTANDING THE REVELATION:
God's Message of Hope for the End Times

Regal Books
A Division of Gospel Light
Ventura, California, U.S.A.

Published by Regal Books
A Division of GL Publications
Ventura, California 93006
Printed in U.S.A.

Library of Congress Cataloging in Publication Data

Vigeveno, H. S.
    In the eye of the apocalypse:understanding the Revelation, God's mes-
sage of hope for the end times/Henk S. Vigeveno.
        p.   cm.
    ISBN 0-8307-1364-6
    1. Bible. N.T. Revelation—Commentaries. I. Title.
BS2825.3.V48   1990
228'.07—dc20   90-31017
                                                                    CIP

1 2 3 4 5 6 7 8 9 10 /X/KP/ 95 94 93 92 91 90

Rights for publishing this book in other languages are contracted by
Gospel Literature International (GLINT) foundation. GLINT also provides technical help for the adaptation, translation, and publishing of
Bible study resources and books in scores of languages worldwide. For
further information, contact GLINT, P.O. Box 488, Rosemead, California,
91770, U.S.A., or the publisher.

THE BOOK OF REVELATION FOR EVERYONE

Read and Understand

"Blessed is the one who reads the words of this prophecy, and blessed are those who hear it and take to heart what is written in it, because the time is near."

REVELATION 1:3

Contents

Introducing Revelation

Like many other Christians, I have shied away from the book of Revelation. Seldom have I read it, even less preached from it—except for an occasional funeral, when I read from the final chapters about the new heaven and the new earth.

For many Christians, like myself, the book of Revelation has been a closed book, probably because the message seems unintelligible and the meaning obscure. Who can understand it? And even if we can understand some of it, isn't Revelation full of doom and judgment? Who wants to read about earthquakes, plagues, horror and destruction? Is that uplifting? Inspiring? Isn't all that doom the very opposite of the gospel of joy and salvation which is the heart of the New Testament?

As a result, the book of Revelation has often remained in the hands of those who preach hellfire and damnation. Or it has fallen to those who decode every verse with Bible-pounding fanaticism. These are the people who explain or attempt to interpret every number, symbol and figure of speech, and who point categorically to events which are now occurring or will soon take place.

All of which leaves other Christians cold as a

cucumber. Why? Because these shenanigans raise the question: How can anyone be sure that his or her interpretation is the right one? And furthermore, what is the point of telling the Christians of the first century that the beast will rise out of the sea in the twentieth?

As I studied several commentaries on the book of Revelation, I discovered an interesting phenomenon. (There are numerous commentaries; only a full-time professor or scholar can begin to read them all.) What I discovered was that writers often contradict one another. Commentators disagree with each other, and they disagree dogmatically.

One writer, for instance, may be absolutely certain that the rider on the white horse is Christ. Who else would ride a *white* horse? he demands. And he advances solid arguments from Scripture to prove his point with reasonable logic. Another commentator is just as certain that the same horse does *not* bring Christ, but the very opposite—war and death. And this commentator marshals a number of reasons to show why this is the only way to explain the passage.

Unsuspecting Christians who read Revelation will experience many difficulties, especially if they peruse more than one book on the text. Sometimes the authors agree, but often they present different interpretations and sometimes far-out views—all with persuasive arguments.

In the light of all these contradictions, what are we to do with Revelation? My response was to study it for myself and to try to develop a unified, integrated view. For some time now I have been studying Revelation to find out what this book is about, and I have been teaching it to other Christians. I now firmly believe that the book of Revelation has been included in the holy Scriptures for a purpose. I have not always lived up to that belief. But I now believe it is time to put what I perceive to be the word of God from the book of Revelation in language which the average Christian can understand—and benefit from!

In attempting to make the book of Revelation readable for everyone, I am not writing a complete commentary. There are enough commentaries already. I am not concerned with interpreting every detail perfectly, but rather with presenting the meaning of the whole. Don't expect to have everything neatly tied up, like a perfectly wrapped present.

What is my purpose then? I hope to give you an idea what the book of Revelation is all about, what its message really is, how it spoke to the early Christians and how it can speak to us today. As you read, I believe you will be amazed to discover the message which the writer intended for all who decipher his book. That in itself is enough of a goal. The book of Revelation is thoroughly Christian. It is important for every age, for every believer. It is full of promise, hope, faith and encouragement!

Having therefore laid my cards on the table, I want to summarize the four major interpretations of the book of Revelation, just so you may know how scholars and others have explained it. Then we will be ready to proceed:

(1) *The Contemporary Interpretation.* This view has sometimes been called the "Preterist" view, but I want to avoid big words which not everyone (including myself) understands! The contemporary interpretation makes the book of Revelation speak only to the first century. According to those who perceive the

book in this way, the writer is writing only for the churches of Asia Minor during the early Christian Era. The judgments he describes took place with the fall of Jerusalem (A.D. 70). And his end-time prophecies point to the fall of the Roman empire (A.D. 476).

(2) *The Historical Interpretation.* Those who hold to a historical interpretation of Revelation explain that the book has been fulfilled in the unfolding history of the Church. Revelation unveils what was about to happen in Christendom through the popes, the Reformation and emperors from Charlemagne to Mussolini. The Spirit of God is informing the early Church with a detailed description of coming events. This raises the question: Why? What good did such prior information accomplish for the first-century Christians?

(3) *The Futuristic Interpretation.* After the opening chapters of Revelation, the writer sees "a door standing open in heaven," and he is summoned to "come up." He is then invited to see "what must take place after this" (Rev. 4:1). Futurists explain that, from this point on, everything described in Revelation refers to what will take place at the end of the present age, prior to and following the second coming of Christ. For the futurist, everything in Revelation after chapter 4 is in the future: tribulation, devastation, judgment, millennium, Kingdom. But this view raises the same question we asked about the previous interpretation: What was the point for the early Christians if everything from chapter 4 on is about the end of the world?

(4) *The Symbolic Interpretation.* Those who explain Revelation symbolically fail to see any *literal* meaning in the verses; they hold to a spiritual interpretation. The book is perceived as idealistic and representative.

For example, the judgment, the second death and hellfire are all seen as symbols and figures of speech.

I refuse to become locked into any one of these positions. I want to take the best of each of these points of view and proceed to what I believe are more important questions: Why was the book of Revelation written? What was the overriding purpose? What is the message of Revelation for us today?

Certainly, Revelation was written to and for the early Christians. That is why it contained primary meaning for them. But some time later, when Church leaders compiled the New Testament (which we believe was done under the guidance of the Holy Spirit), the book of Revelation was included. Why? Because it had a message not only for the first century or for the twentieth, but *for all Christians* throughout the history of the Church. That is why the book was included in the Bible. That is why the Church leaders believed it was the inspired Word of God.

What, then, is that message?

Consider this: The book of Revelation is predominately a book of comfort. It asserts that even though "all hell breaks loose," God is still on His throne. The Lord is sovereign. He is sovereign right now! His reign and His victory are assured. That is why Christians need not fear. The eternal purpose of God is centered in the Church. The Church will not be defeated, even though she is severely tested. The beast may arise from the sea and the harlot-city will seduce many, but neither the beast nor the harlot will be forever. Only God is forever.

The Lord will establish His Kingdom. The Church is the focus of the Kingdom. He is King of kings and Lord of lords!

That, in brief, is the message of Revelation. I agree with William Hendricksen, whose commentary on Revelation has gone through twenty-five printings. He wrote: "The purpose of the Book of Revelation is to comfort the militant Church in its struggle against the forces of evil."[1]

CHAPTER ONE

The Lord of the Church

Revelation 1

The revelation of Jesus Christ, which God gave him to show his servants what must soon take place (Rev. 1:1).

This is the revelation of Jesus Christ—not of John. It is Jesus Christ who is revealed, who is the center of this book.

A revelation is an unveiling, like removing the covering of a statue so that the work of art may be seen. And what is being unveiled? Jesus Christ. Yes, the book is full of shocking disclosures about judgments which will come on the earth. But the book should not be called "Revelations." The title is in the singular. This is the revelation of Jesus Christ.

There were many fortune-tellers, astrologers and soothsayers in the first century, far more proportionately than in our time. Against this background of those who supposedly unveiled hidden things, the book of Revelation reveals the True!

John, the Author

He made it known by sending his angel to his servant John, who testifies to everything he saw–that is, the word of God and the testimony of Jesus Christ (1:1,2).

Most interpreters do not dispute that John, the apostle, is the author of the Revelation. In the text, he identifies himself only as "John," and he calls himself a servant rather than an apostle. (With modesty and humility, he shuns titles.) Many writers also agree that this is the same John who wrote the Gospel and the New Testament letters. This includes the church father Irenaeus, who as a boy knew the martyr Polycarp, who in turn knew John—as well as Justin Martyr (A.D. 135), Jerome, Augustine, Ambrose and many others.

The revelation of Jesus Christ is the Word of God. It is also the testimony of Jesus Christ. This means the book of Revelation is authentic truth. Prophecy: "Thus says the Lord."

Blessed is the one who reads the words of this prophecy, and blessed are those who hear it and take to heart what is written in it, because the time is near (1:3).

Here is the first blessing, or beatitude, of the book. There are seven beatitudes. The blessing is for anyone who reads and ponders the Word of God. The book of Revelation is not to be shunned, as has often happened in Christendom. (The quotable and insightful commentator J. A. Bengel thinks that many Christians believe verse 3 reads: "Blessed are those who do *not* read this book," since they avoid it like the plague.)

Revelation is to be read not for curiosity but for comprehension, for spiritual guidance and strength, because "the time is near." It was near for the early Church, and it is near for us. The nearness of "the end" has been an emphasis throughout Christian history. The coming of the Kingdom is a promise and *always* an imminent possibility. If we believe the Revelation of Jesus, we will look for the return of our Lord.

What John has written as "revelation" is also called "prophecy." We tend to limit the word "prophecy" to something that will happen in the future. But Bible prophecy is about the present as well as the future—about what God wills done as well as what God will do. Prophecy is for now and then, for insight and foresight.

Revelation—unveiling, uncovering.

Prophecy—insight and foresight.

The Greeting

This book of prophecy begins with a conventional greeting, an address to the churches:

> *John, to the seven churches in the province of Asia: Grace and peace to you...(1:4).*

"Grace" is the Greek greeting; "peace," the Jewish. Thus John is addressing Christians both from the Greek world (Gentiles) and from the Jewish heritage. And he greets them in the name of the one God in three person: Father, Son and Holy Spirit:

From him who is, and who was, and who is to come.

This refers to God the Father.

...and from the seven spirits before his throne ...

This is a reference to the Holy Spirit, who is also known as the sevenfold Spirit. The reference is to the perfection or the holiness of the Spirit. As we will see, the number seven is used throughout the book of Revelation to symbolize perfection.

...and from Jesus Christ, who is the faithful witness, the firstborn from the dead, and the ruler of the kings of the earth (1:5).

With the last part of this verse, the unveiling of Jesus Christ begins.

The Unveiling

Jesus is the One who was approved as a faithful witness in His life and ministry.

Through His resurrection, He became the firstborn from the dead.

He is Lord of all. Right now He reigns on the throne. And He will be recognized as Lord when He comes again!

The unveiling of Christ is the unveiling of the Son of man, who lived in the flesh, died on the cross, rose from the dead and sits on the throne as Ruler of all. Jesus is Lord. We have nothing to fear if we believe in the Lord who will always be in control!

*To him who loves us and has freed us from our sins
by his blood ...(1:5).*

This refers to the atonement. Christ has died for
us—we are saved! Throughout the book of
Revelation, we will be reminded of this salvation He
has brought us. We need the reassurance of our salvation through Jesus Christ as we confront the trials that
will test us.

In fact, we are more than "saved":

*...and has made us to be a kingdom and priests to
serve his God and Father—to him be glory and
power for ever and ever! Amen (1:6).*

Freed from sin, we are to be God's people. We have
been called to rule as kings and to serve as priests. In
the Old Testament, those who were kings could not be
priests, and those who served as priests could not be
kings. Kings came from one tribe, priests from another. Jesus Christ alone was and is both King of kings
and High Priest. And we, as His people, are now
called *both* kings and priests. This is certainly an
encouraging word for Christians who feel neglected
and rejected by the world!

This introduction to the book of Revelation mounts
to a paean of praise before the disclosure of Jesus
Christ continues:

*Look, he is coming with the clouds,
   and every eye will see him,
     even those who pierced him;
   and all the peoples of the earth
     will mourn because of him.
        So shall it be! Amen (1:7).*

Jesus Christ is the hope of the Christian and the revelation of God to the whole world. This verse, which describes that moment of recognition that turns into pain for those who have not believed, is a quotation from Zechariah 12:10—one of many echoes of the Old Testament in Revelation. The honored scholars and New Testament compilers B. F. Westcott and F. J. A. Hort list nearly 400 references and allusions to the Old Testament in the book of Revelation. John does not copy verse after verse from other prophets, but he is visibly influenced by the imagery of Scripture, which is his heritage as a Jew. It is impossible to avoid this fact—the book of Revelation leans heavily on the Old Testament.

> "I am the Alpha and the Omega," says the Lord God, "who is, and who was, and who is to come, the Almighty" (1:8).

Alpha and Omega—A to Z. The Lord is at the beginning (Creation) and He is at the end (Kingdom). He is also present everywhere between, including B, C, D, and R, S, T. The Lord is sovereign even now. That is His revelation to us!

He is the Almighty. Only once in the other books of the New Testament is God called the Almighty. In the book of Revelation He is called "the Almighty" eight times. For Christians living in a hostile world, this is helpful reassurance.

Divine Inspiration

> I, John, your brother and companion...

The writer identifies himself with us. He again

shuns the title of apostle, stressing that he is a servant of the Lord and our brother in Christ.

...in the suffering and kingdom and patient endurance that are ours in Jesus ...

In Jesus we experience both suffering and the Kingdom, both perseverance and permanence.

...was on the island of Patmos because of the word of God and the testimony of Jesus (1:9).

Patmos is a small island off the Mediterranean coast near Ephesus. In all probability, John was banished there during a time of persecution.

The identification of the Word of God with the testimony of Jesus (as in v. 2), underlines the divinity of Jesus and the authority of his Word.

It was on the Lord's day, and I was caught up by the Spirit; and behind me I heard a loud voice, like the sound of a trumpet, which said to me, "Write down what you see on a scroll and send it to the seven churches: to Ephesus, Smyrna, Pergamum, Thyatira, Sardis, Philadelphia, and Laodicea" (1:10,11, NEB).

The Lord's day is the day of resurrection, the day on which the early Christians worshiped.

And the message given on this Lord's day is clear. The churches are called by name.

The seven cities listed in verse 11 were prominent in Asia Minor at the time Revelation was written. Ephesus was the largest, situated on the coast of the

Aegean Sea. Smyrna lay on the coast northward, and the others formed something of a circle—north, east, south and then west, back to Ephesus. They were united by a postal system and came under a central judicial administration. In this book John connects the established fellowships, the home churches of Christians in each community.

> *I turned around to see the voice that was speaking to me. And when I turned I saw seven gold lampstands (1:12).*

The speaker is invisible—all John sees are seven lampstands. Later, in verse 20, he is told that these lampstands represent the seven churches to which he is about to write.

Jesus Revealed

> *And among the lampstands was someone "like a son of man," dressed in a robe reaching down to his feet and with a golden sash around his chest. His head and hair were white like wool, as white as snow, and his eyes were like blazing fire. His feet were like bronze glowing in a furnace, and his voice was like the sound of rushing waters. In his right hand he held seven stars, and out of his mouth came a sharp double-edged sword. His face was like the sun shining in all its brilliance (1:13-16).*

Jesus Christ is with, among and in the churches. He was there among the churches clustered around Ephesus, and He is now present in every part of our world. He abides not only in Asia, but also in Europe, the Americas, Africa—everywhere. He may be found in large churches or small and in home fellow-ships—wherever two or three gather in His name. That is the assurance conveyed by this vision.

The unveiling of Jesus Christ:

He is human, "son of man," like us.

He wears a priestly robe. He is our High Priest. He intercedes for us.

White hair? Why? Has Jesus aged? No. White stands not only for purity, but also for the wisdom of the ages.

His eyes are like fire. They penetrate—searing, searching.

His feet are like bronze—strong, trampling down the enemy.

His voice is like rushing waters—awesome, majes-tic. Terrible to His foes, it is pleasant to those who believe in Him—like music to our ears!

The sword from His mouth is the Word and testi-mony of Jesus Christ—sharp, and with the double edge of grace and judgment.

His face is like the sun. He is transfigured in glory.

In His right hand He holds seven stars, which He will soon reveal as the "angels" or messengers of the seven churches (1:20). Christ holds the leaders of His church in His hands. The Lord is in control, even though we may not always be aware of it.

"When I saw him, I fell at his feet as though dead."

Roman subjects fell at the feet of Roman emperors and worshiped them as gods—the scene was familiar for the early Church. But to the writer of Revelation, Jesus Christ alone is worthy of our worship. He alone is Lord. Among the apostles and early Christians, there is no hesitation about according worship to Jesus Christ!

> *But he laid his right hand upon me and said, "Do not be afraid. I am the first and the last, and I am the living one; for I was dead and now I am alive for evermore, and I hold the keys of Death and Death's domain" (1:17,18, NEB).*

The unveiling of Jesus Christ continues. He calms His servant John and tells him not to be afraid. Why should we not fear? Because Jesus is the Alpha and Omega, the first and the Last, even as the Father is the first and the Last (v. 8). He has come from God and *is* God (John.1:1). He died for us and He rose again. He is alive forevermore. We have nothing to fear because the risen Savior holds the keys of death and death's domain—literally "Hades," the realm of the dead. Death cannot hurt anyone who trusts in Him.

The risen Lord has overcome the enemy. That is why we need not be afraid. The unknown (death) has been unmasked. We trust in Him who has made the journey and returned triumphant!

Write the Message

> *Write, therefore, what you have seen, what is now and what will take place later. The mystery of the seven stars that you saw in my right hand and of the seven golden lampstands is this: The seven stars are the angels [messengers] of the seven churches, and the seven lampstands are the seven churches (1:19,20).*

The book of Revelation is inspired. If we are to believe John, we understand that John did not create this book. It was given to him by means of voice and vision. John is instructed to be faithful to that Word and to write it down. Because he obeyed, we hold the book in our hands.

One word of caution concerning "what you have seen, what is now and what will take place later." This has an explicit, precise sound, but it is neither explicit nor precise. We live in a culture that prides itself on scientific precision and computer accuracy. And so we expect Revelation to be a progressive, orderly account that will propel us from the present toward the new heaven and the new earth. We want it to be a reasonable statement about events which will follow one another until everything is completed. It is not!

The book of Revelation is not an exhibit of precise photographs. It is rather a collection of impressionist or even abstract paintings, some of which may be hard to decipher, especially at close range. Like the best modern art, these visions have a powerful impact and a ring of truth—truth that perhaps could not be conveyed through more "rational" form. But they are hardly precise. They are vivid impressions of things to come.

That is not to say that the message of Revelation is unintelligible. It brings a forceful message about what is *now* and what will be—the present and the future. With that much information, we can proceed to interpret the book.

We are living in a time when the visitation of God is near. There may be trials and tribulations for the Church in the world, but we have nothing to fear. Jesus Christ is Lord. And He has in His possession the keys of death and death's domain.

Questions for Discussion and Meditation

1. Does the Revelation of Jesus harmonize or differ from the Jesus of the Gospels?

2. What, if anything, *new* do you discover about Jesus in the book of Revelation?

3. How does John's description of himself affect your view of "being a Christian"?

4. In what practical way are we already "a kingdom and priests"?

CHAPTER TWO

The Message to the Church

Revelation 2 and 3

The Revelation of Jesus Christ is for the Church. In chapter 1 of the book of Revelation, John has greeted the seven churches in Asia Minor. Now, in the next two chapters, he relays to each church a specific message.

How shall we interpret these chapters?

The initial meaning is clear. John writes specifically to the seven churches in Asia Minor. Every church is addressed separately and is commended, instructed, sometimes reprimanded but always encouraged. Yet surely the communication to the seven churches has a wider appeal, just as Paul's letters to the Romans, Corinthians, Galatians and Ephesians speak to all of us!

Does each of these churches represent a specific period of history from the first century to the twentieth? Can we project their situations into stages of church history? Not necessarily. Those who decode

Revelation as preview history have applied these chapters to popes, protestants and unorthodox sects. In their view, for example, the church of Philadelphia symbolizes the missionary movement of the nineteenth century and the church of Laodicea parallels the lukewarm church of our time.

In my opinion, this strains the original text. It forces an unnatural load on the initial meaning. I believe it is much better to read the letters to the seven churches with application for today. Some churches fit one situation, some another. What is most helpful is to conceive of these chapters like this: *The conditions of the seven churches are always present!* Approaching the Bible with this perception will help us to discern the Word of God for our churches today!

The Church at Ephesus

To the angel of the church in Ephesus write: ...

Ephesus was a major commercial center on the Aegean Sea. The city was influential in Asia Minor, boasting a large marketplace, a theater seating 25,000 and a temple to the goddess Diana with 127 marble pillars, 36 of which were overlaid with gold. The church of Ephesus was very influential. Timothy, to whom Paul wrote two New Testament letters, was the pastor. According to tradition, the mother of Jesus had been a member and John, now a senior citizen, was a quiet and respected leader.

> *These are the words of him who holds the seven stars in his right hand and walks among the seven golden lampstands (2:1).*

Jesus is the Lord of the church. He controls the pastors (stars), and He walks among the churches (lampstands). Jesus is always among us in the life and worship of the church. He is present with us!

I know your deeds, your hard work and your perseverance. I know that you cannot tolerate wicked men, that you have tested those who claim to be apostles but are not, and have found them false. You have persevered and have endured hardships for my name, and have not grown weary (2:1-3).

Jesus knows what is happening in the Church. He is aware of everything. Nothing is hidden from His eyes. Do we believe this? When we utterly believe and trust the living Lord, the Church of Jesus Christ will experience renewal!

Jesus commends the Ephesian church for spiritual good works. The struggles and patience of the Christians are not lost to our Lord. Twice in this passage He mentions their works and their perseverance. To keep the faith while we are severely tried is worthy of praise. In Ephesus the Church tested its Christian leaders. Those who denied the centrality of the faith were disciplined.

But all is not well in this large, thriving church. (Can things sometimes be amiss in today's vital megachurches?)

Yet I hold this against you: You have forsaken your first love. Remember the height from which you have fallen! Repent and do the things you did at first (2:4,5).

Jesus counsels us: "Seek first the kingdom of God" (Matt. 6:33, NKJV). The Kingdom is to be our "first love." And yet most of us have times when our first love cools. Once we experienced great fervor for the Kingdom. Our relationship with Christ was new and vital. We were enthusiastic, yes, filled with the Spirit. And now? What has happened? What idol has crowded out everything else in our hearts? We were so close to the Lord that we were "high," but we have fallen from that height. We have lost the initial excitement of walking with God.

It is very dangerous to continue in this casual manner. Something must be done! In this passage, Jesus directs us concerning two things:

(1) *Remember how fervently you believed when you first became a Christian.* You were "in love." You were a different person. You felt like a new person! You were excited about your faith. Do you remember? Bring up the past on the screen of your mind. This will help you to return to your initial love!

(2) *Repent of your ways.* Turn around. Change direction. Humble yourself in the sight of the Lord, and He will lift you up.

> *If you do not repent, I will come to you and remove your lampstand from its place.*

Serious consequences—if we do not heed the word of truth! Our church will be removed! Even a great church like the one in Ephesus can fall—and how great a fall! How often has it happened since this message was first given to John on Patmos?

A lamp needs no stand when the light has gone out.

*But you have this in your favor: You hate the prac-
tices of the Nicolaitans, which I also hate. He who
has an ear, let him hear what the Spirit says to the
churches (2:6,7).*

Who were the Nicolaitans? John was probably
using a "cover" for a serious problem in the first century. Some think the Nicolaitans describes the
Gnostics, a liberal sect which identified matter as evil
and spirit as good. They lived very free lives, including the sharing of goods and wives. In a larger sense,
the Nicolaitans represent the world in which we live,
the permissive society. Jesus also hated this sect for
their misinterpretation and misapplication of His
Word.

"He who has an ear, let him hear what the Spirit
says to the churches" is repeated seven times, once to
every church. Since the command is so frequent, we
need to underline it. Are we attentive to Jesus? Do we
hear the Word which is personally addressed to us?
We have the physical apparatuses (ears, hearing aids,
eyes, glasses). Are we using them as they were
designed to be used? The Holy Spirit is always talking
to the Church. His message is vital to our well-being.

*To him who overcomes, I will give the right to eat
from the tree of life, which is in the paradise of God
(2:7).*

The one who persists in faith until the end will join
in the victory of our Lord. The person who holds on is
an "overcomer" and will have access to the tree of life.
This tree was in the paradise of Eden. It awaits us in
"the paradise of God," the eternal city described later

in Revelation 22:2. This is the tree of eternal life.

The Church at Smyrna

To the angel of the church in Smyrna write: ...

Smyrna was a sizable city of 200,000, a trade center with a busy harbor. It boasted a large library, a stadium, and a theater.

> *These are the words of him who is the first and the Last, who died and came to life again (2:8).*

The Lord who speaks to this church is the One from the beginning, the One who will be there at the end. He has declared Himself as the Alpha and Omega, the parentheses of history. All human history is played out between these opening and closing parentheses, between the *A* and the *Z*.

He is the Savior who died on the cross, the victorious Lord who rose from the dead. When the Church endures persecution in the world, the Cross and the Resurrection are our only hope!

> *I know your afflictions and your poverty—yet you are rich! I know the slander of those who say they are Jews and are not, but are a synagogue of Satan. Do not be afraid of what you are about to suffer. I tell you, the devil will put some of you in prison to test you, and you will suffer persecution for ten days (2:9,10).*

Everything is positive for this church! Christians survived terrible oppression in Smyrna, but they withstood and will continue to resist the assault. And in His message to Smyrna, Jesus reveals to us the continuing lot of the church—testing from the world and from the devil.

Some of our trials will come from those who resist the gospel and claim to be true to tradition: "They say they are Jews." That is, they rely on the law. "Those who say they are Jews" can represent any religion which teaches that heaven is gained by good works. Dependence on the works of the law is the opposite of acceptance of the grace of God. The conclusion we draw from Revelation is that those who are not of God belong to Satan.

"Ten days." Ten what? Literal days? Symbolic days? Ten years of Roman persecution? Who can be sure? The meaning of "ten" in this context is probably not a specific number but "a limited time." We need not force the text into a literal ten days. The message is that Christians may be tested for an indefinite but regulated time. Jesus knows everything. He is always in control! We need never fear, no matter how intense our suffering. Jesus expects us to remain faithful.

> *Be faithful, even to the point of death, and I will give you the crown of life. He who has an ear, let him hear what the Spirit says to the churches. He who overcomes will not be hurt at all by the second death (2:10-11).*

The one who persists in faith until the end will receive a crown of life. A crown can be gold or brass or of a definite shape, but what is "a crown of life"? "Crown" is surely meant symbolically. Our reward is to be crowned (spiritually speaking) with eternal life!

The first death is physical, the second death spiritual. The second death means eternal separation from God (see Rev. 20:14).

The Church at Pergamum

To the angel of the church in Pergamum write: ...

"Pergamum" means "citadel"–a fortress or stronghold. The city had an altar to Zeus and a temple dedicated to Caesar Augustus. Another temple was dedicated to Asclepios, the god of healing.

These are the words of him who has the sharp, double-edged sword (2:12).

The Lord who speaks to this church is the perceptive Lord who divides the true from the false. In this center of paganism, the Christian Church needed that kind of discernment. The sword is the Word of God (Heb. 4:12). The double edge depicts grace and judgment.

I know where you live; it is the place where Satan has his throne (2:13, NEB).

Jesus not only knows what is happening in the Church. He also understands the society which surrounds us. The secular city is the heathen city, and its idols are condemned by the one and only Lord. Idols are not of God. Therefore they must be of Satan (see John 8:44). Satan rules in the pagan culture.

And yet you are holding fast to my cause. You did not deny your faith in me even at the time when Antipas, my faithful witness, was killed in your city, the home of Satan (2:13, NEB).

Christians are encouraged to remain true to Jesus Christ. We may be called upon to become martyrs (like Antipas). If we believe Jesus Christ is Lord, we cannot deny Him. If we confess Him in the hostile world, He will also confess us in heaven! (see Matt. 10:32).

Satan lives in your city. Jesus lives in your church.

Nevertheless, I have a few things against you: You have people there who hold to the teaching of Balaam, who taught Balak to entice the Israelites to sin by eating food sacrificed to idols and by committing sexual immorality. Likewise you also have those who hold to the teaching of the Nicolaitans (2:14,15).

When Christians veer from the truth, they stray from the narrow way. Sometimes they follow in the footsteps of Balaam, a prophet from Moab who persuaded the king of Moab (Balak) to use women of low morals to seduce Israel. How readily can Christians be tempted! The seduction to worldliness and immorality (Nicolaitans) attacks us everywhere.

Repent therefore! Otherwise, I will soon come to you and will fight against them with the sword of my mouth (2:16).

Any Christian who falls is able to repent. That is all

we can do. And we will be made whole. Even Balaamites and Nicolaitans can be forgiven. They are welcome when they return to God! Without repentance and confession, only the judgment side of the sword remains.

The faithful who resist the seduction of false teaching and practice, as well as those who repent from their excursions into paganism, will receive rewards:

> *He who has an ear, let him hear what the Spirit says to the churches. To him who overcomes, I will give some of the hidden manna. I will also give him a white stone with a new name written on it, known only to him who receives it (2:17).*

The manna of the Old Testament is the Bread of Life of the New, the bread that came down from heaven. Jesus Christ is that manna. We will receive the satisfying Bread of eternal life. But why is this manna "hidden"? It is hidden from the world. It is hidden from those who fail to repent of their sinful deeds.

The white stone is like a ticket of admission, a special pass that gets you into "those parties." In the world you need an invitation before you can enter certain places. A *white* stone (white for purity) is your ticket of admission to the party God will throw, the banquet of heaven. All who hear what the Spirit is saying to the churches and respond are invited to attend!

And all who hear and respond will receive a new name as well—just as Abram became Abraham, as Jacob was renamed Israel, as Saul became Paul. The new name means a new creation, becoming a new person in Christ (2 Cor. 5:17).

The Church at Thyatira

To the angel of the church at Thyatira write:...

Thyatira was a city of merchants and craftsmen. It was important to belong to "the workers union." If you were not a member of the guild, you were exposed to persecution. You would surely experience social isolation and financial pressure.

> *These are the words of the Son of God, whose eyes are like blazing fire and whose feet are like burnished bronze (2:18).*

This is the Christ revealed in the first chapter—a figure with piercing eyes and feet that trample down the enemies of God. He comes to the Church with that penetrating vision, with eyes that look right through us and see our hidden agendas. He comes to purify the Church. He is the Son of God.

> *I know your deeds, your love and faith, your service and perseverance, and that you are now doing more than you did at first (2:19).*

Nothing is lost to the Lord, who knows and sees all. There are Christians, like those in Thyatira, who will be highly commended because they are constantly growing in their faith. They are doing more now than they did at the beginning of their pilgrimage. Instead of losing their first love, they have extended their commitment!

But not all is well in Thyatira:

Nevertheless, I have this against you: You tolerate that woman Jezebel, who calls herself a prophetess. By her teaching she misleads my servants into sexual immorality and the eating of food sacrificed to idols. I have given her time to repent of her immorality, but she is unwilling. So I will cast her on a bed of suffering, and I will make those who commit adultery with her suffer intensely, unless they repent of her ways. I will strike her children dead. Then all the churches will know that I am he who searches hearts and minds, and I will repay each of you according to your deeds (2:20-23).

It is doubtful that a woman named "Jezebel" actually lived in Thyatira. The name is a deliberate choice, a reference to the Old Testament Jezebel, King Ahab's wife. She was a powerful, evil woman and an idolatress. She controlled her husband and her country and led Israel astray (see 1 Kings 16-21, 2 Kings 9). She was the epitome of evil in the Old Testament.

Why does John speak of Jezebel to this Church? Quite likely, he refers to a false teaching which could well be named "Jezebel" because of its immorality and idolatry. Then who would Jezebel's children be? Those who follow false doctrine and live "worldly" lives!

One thing is clear. The Lord is in charge of the church—not Jezebel, the seductress, the evil woman. False teaching and lies may prevail in some churches, but they will not endure. The Lord comes to purify the Church.

The depiction of her punishment is graphic. Jezebel, the adulteress, will be lying in a bed, but not a pleasure bed. Hers will be a sickbed, a bed of suffering. Judgment is the result of spiritual adultery and folly!

> *Now I say to the rest of you in Thyatira, to you who do not hold to her teaching and have not learned Satan's so-called deep secrets (I will not impose any other burden on you): Only hold on to what you have until I come. To him who overcomes and does my will to the end I will give authority over the nations—*
>
> *"He will rule them with an iron scepter;*
> *he will dash them to pieces like pottery"*
>
> *just as I have received authority from my Father. I will also give him the morning star. He who has an ear, let him hear what the Spirit says to the churches (2:24-29).*

This is the message from the Lord for us. Do the will of the Lord! Do not stray from the truth! Trust in Jesus Christ! Hold on until the very end. Live in hope for the salvation which will be brought us at the appearing of Jesus Christ!

The promise to those who persevere in the faith is "authority." We will be given "authority" to rule. The meek will "inherit the earth" (see Ps. 37:11, Matt. 5:5). The valleys (the lowly) will be exalted, while the mountains (the mighty) will be leveled (see Isa. 40:4).

What is the morning star? Some say the planet Venus, which during certain times of year is the last bright heavenly body to fade at dawn. Caesar's legions carried the sign of Venus on their standards as a symbol of conquest. Christians will receive "the morning star" because they serve the living Lord who has conquered death and the grave. Rome will fade away, but Christians who secure "the morning star" will participate with Christ in His victory!

The Church at Sardis

To the angel of the church in Sardis write:...

Sardis was a city basking in past glories. Gold had been discovered there long before, but Sardis would eventually become like a ghost town in the American West. In New Testament times, the city enjoyed a reputation which it did not deserve, since it was in rapid decline.

These are the words of him who holds the seven spirits of God and the seven stars (3:1).

"The seven spirits of God" represents the Holy Spirit. (Throughout the book of Revelation, the number seven means perfect and complete.) Jesus promised the Holy Spirit to the disciples to lead them into all truth. The Lord of truth now speaks through the Spirit. And He reminds us that He holds the leaders of the church (seven stars) in His hands.

I know your deeds; you have a reputation of being alive, but you are dead. Wake up! Strengthen what remains and is about to die, for I have not found your deeds complete in the sight of my God. Remember, therefore, what you have received and heard; obey it, and repent. But if you do not wake up, I will come like a thief, and you will not know at what time I will come to you (3:1-3).

The situation in the church echoes that of the declining city! And it may be our situation as well! Is our church dead or alive, asleep or awake? We may believe ourselves to be awake when we are actually in dreamland! If we are spiritually asleep, can we be stirred out of dullness and apathy? Does anything remain from before we became drowsy? Reinforce your faith, your beliefs, your works—now!

Two familiar words are spoken to this church:

(1) *Remember.* Recall to memory the good news of Jesus Christ. You will be saved by your memory when you return to Him! Hear and obey the word of the Lord!

(2) *Repent.* Turn from your incomplete deeds to the forgiving Lord. He will accept you. Wake up out of your stupor, or else you will be surprised by the return of the Lord. He will arrive when you do not expect Him, just as a thief breaks into your home without previous announcement.

> *Yet you have a few people in Sardis who have not soiled their clothes. They will walk with me, dressed in white, for they are worthy. He who overcomes will, like them, be dressed in white. I will never blot out his name from the book of life, but will acknowledge his name before my Father and his angels. He who has an ear, let him hear what the Spirit says to the churches (3:4-6).*

Even in a dead church there can be live Christians.

Even among those who have soiled their clothes there surface those who are clean by the word Jesus has spoken (see John 15:3). They are worthy who are called worthy by Jesus Christ. Worthiness is no human accomplishment. Worthiness is the gift of grace from the One who has died for us. Only Jesus Christ can wash our filthy clothes clean. Only He pronounces us worthy.

We are even assured that our names are written in the book of life. God is in charge of that book. When we accept Jesus as our Lord and Savior *and He accepts us,* our names are written down, never to be erased. This is our assurance from His Word.

The Church in Philadelphia

To the angel of the church in Philadelphia write: ...

Volcanic eruptions and earthquakes hampered the commercial center which was Philadelphia. There were many heathen temples and pagan festivals in the city, and because it was a vine-growing district, the worship of the wine God Dionysus was its chief cult.

> *These are the words of him who is holy and true, who holds the key of David. What he opens no one can shut, and what he shuts no one can open (3:7).*

Jesus Christ is holy. Jesus Christ is the Truth. Jesus Christ is in control. This is how Jesus addresses this church in a secular city. He alone can open the way into the Kingdom or close it. No other person retains that power.

What is "the key of David"? A key means authority. Jesus gave the keys of the Kingdom to the apostles. When they began the proclamation of the gospel, they were granted permission to include or exclude from the Kingdom. But why the key *of David?* David, the king of Israel, was promised that his kingdom would be forever. Jesus was born of the line of David. He is the promised heir to the throne of David, to the eternal Kingdom.

> *I know your deeds. See, I have placed before you an open door that no one can shut. I know that you have little strength, yet you have kept my word and have not denied my name (3:8).*

This door mentioned in this verse has sometimes been interpreted as a door of missions. But the book of Revelation does not state that the door is a missionary opportunity. The letters to the churches concern the Kingdom of God. It is more likely, then, that the door is the door into the Kingdom. Jesus is the Lord who has the authority to allow us into heaven. The door and the way are now open!

Jesus tells us that in ourselves we have little strength to keep the faith. Such strength does not originate in us, but in Him. When we stifle His Spirit, we hurt ourselves. Then, when the test comes, we may deny His name. We need to be empowered by His Spirit in order to remain faithful.

> *I will make those of Satan's synagogue, who claim to be Jews but are lying frauds, come and fall down at your feet; and they shall know that you are my beloved people. Because you have kept my command and stood fast, I will also keep you from the ordeal that is to fall upon the whole world and test its inhabitants (3:9,10, NEB).*

Those who are not of God are of the devil. Those who are not of the truth are liars (see John 8:44). It does not matter what their claims may be. They may even claim "to be Jews" (religious), but they are not. At the appearing of Jesus Christ they will have to acknowledge the true gospel. At that time those who are faithful to Christ will be vindicated. The truth of God will triumph over the lies of men.

There is more. Christians will be kept from "the hour of trial." What hour is this? Is this *one* hour? One month? One year? Seven? Three and a half? Probably, as in the earlier reference to "ten days" (2:10), this "one hour" speaks symbolically of a time of testing for the world. It will be for a limited period only, that is, one hour. And Christians are promised that God's judgments will not afflict His own people!

I am coming soon (3:11).

What is the sense of "soon"? Surely "soon" contained meaning for the early Christians, and it has had significance for Christians throughout the centuries. Without a doubt, "soon" has implications for our age.

In God's time, the coming of the Kingdom is always *soon*. "Soon" implies a few days. If a thousand years are like a day in God's timetable (see 2 Pet. 3:8), 2000 years of Christianity are like two days. Speaking in those terms, our century is within the scope of "soon." Christians have always been alert because of the teaching of Jesus (see Matt. 24–25, Luke 21). They are aware that the return of Christ will be "soon."

In view of this truth, Jesus says, "hold on!":

Hold on to what you have, so that no one will take your crown. Him who overcomes I will make a pillar in the temple of my God. Never again will he leave it. I will write on him the name of my God and the name of the city of my God, the new Jerusalem, which is coming down out of heaven from my God; and I will also write on him my new name. He who has an ear, let him hear what the Spirit says to the churches (3:11-13).

Those who do not deny their faith will "gain a crown," that is, the reward of faithfulness. They will be like pillars in the temple. This does not mean they will be turned into physical pillars, of course. The word "pillar" implies stability, permanence—in the sense that we refer to committed Christians as "pillars of the church."

The city of God which is to be hoped for is also stable, permanent—unlike the city of man, which will pass away.

The new name is the name of salvation. Each follower of Christ is "a new creation" (2 Cor. 5:17), and God assures us we belong to Him. With His name upon us, our identity is in Him!

The letter to the church at Philadelphia, like the one to the church at Smyrna, contains only pluses. There are no reprimands to the Christians in these two cities. They are strongly encouraged to continue to trust, to persevere, to hear the Word and to grow in grace.

The Church at Laodicea

To the angel of the church in Laodicea write: ...

Laodicea was probably the richest of the seven

cities of Asia Minor. The city boasted a prosperous linen and wool industry, as well as a medical center specializing in eye problems. The banks of Laodicea were wealthy institutions.

> *These are the words of the Amen, the faithful and true witness, the ruler of God's creation (3:14).*

The Amen—the One who says, "So be it"—is the Truth.

The faithful and true witness is Jesus in His humanity.

He is also the ruler of God's creation, now and then. Jesus Christ is already on the throne. Rome is not sovereign. Jesus will be revealed as the sovereign Lord in time to come!

The letter to the church at Laodicea includes no commendations whatever! References to good works and Christian service are absent.

> *I know your deeds, that you are neither cold nor hot. I wish you were either one or the other! So, because you are lukewarm—neither hot nor cold—I am about to spit you out of my mouth (3:15,16).*

A cup of hot coffee which has stood around a while and cooled tastes insipid. So does a glass of iced tea which has grown warm. Either gets tossed out as undrinkable. Jesus is more graphic: "I am about to spit you out." Indifference is disgusting. It is better to be hot or cold in our commitment than somewhere in no man's land.

You say, "How rich I am! And how well I have done! I have everything I want." In fact, though you do not know it, you are the most pitiful wretch, poor, blind, and naked. So I advise you to buy from me gold refined in the fire, to make you truly rich, and white clothes to put on to hide the shame of your nakedness, and ointment for your eyes so that you may see (3:17,18, NEB).

Jesus wants us to be aware of our spiritual condition! His words pierce the heart: *"You do not realize."* Are we unaware? Are we fooling ourselves? Do we view our church property and buildings with pride and count our assets while we fail to take stock of our spiritual malaise? Do we dress ourselves in clerical garb but remain naked in terms of righteousness? Are we willing to see ourselves as the Lord sees us? Can we afford to reject this unveiling? What is our response when the truth breaks open in our hearts?

In spite of the blindness of this church, Jesus is very tender: "I counsel you," He says, not "I condemn you." His recommendations are wise. We need to listen. He offers us the gold of spiritual truth which can make us rich toward God. Our dirty laundry will be washed to cover our immoral nakedness. He is willing to provide us with salve (like the eye medicine manufactured in Laodicea) to heal our distorted vision. Only then will we perceive spiritual truth.

Those whom I love I rebuke and discipline. So be earnest, and repent (3:19).

Jesus' tone remains tender, not harsh or angry. He is not angry with us. He counsels us for our good. We are encouraged to be in earnest—to become serious about our faith. We can no longer play at Christianity!

> *Here I stand knocking at the door; if anyone hears my voice and opens the door, I will come in and sit down to supper with him and he with me (3:20, NEB).*

He who walks among the churches stands outside of this church. In the sanctuary, Christians lustily sing praises to the Lord, but the Lord is not inside. The first thing this church needs to do, therefore, is invite Jesus in. When He is invited to enter, He will come not simply as the Savior Who will eat with us, but as the Lord Who bids us to His table!

Jesus says, "I stand at the door and knock," to all lukewarm churches. He also stands at the door (the heart, the will) of individuals. He comes often. He may be there now, at your door!

> *To him who overcomes, I will give the right to sit with me on my throne, just as I overcame and sat down with my Father on his throne. He who has an ear, let him hear what the Spirit says to the churches (3:21,22).*

When lukewarm Christians repent and "get hot," they are assured the promises of God! Like the prodigal son, who came home to a fun party, insipid and sinful Christians are invited by our Savior to a wonderful welcome celebration. His promise is for all who hear the Word of God and do it.

And what a promise—to sit with Jesus on His throne! Can it be true? Is this the reward for those

Christians who were severely chastised for their luke-warm apathy? Yes. There is hope for all. Hear what the Spirit is saying to you today!

Questions for Discussion and Meditation

1. What is the Lord's essential message to *all* the churches mentioned in these two chapters?

2. "Hear what the Spirit says to the churches."

   (a) What does this say about the inspiration of Scripture?

   (b) How is Scripture to be read?

3. What do you see that the first- and twentieth-century Christians may have in common?

4. What encouragement do you discover for yourself from the messages to the seven churches?

CHAPTER THREE

The Vision of Heaven

Revelation 4 and 5

As the instruction to the seven churches concludes, the revelation of Jesus Christ resumes with a glorious vision! We are transported to heaven. Jesus Christ is more fully revealed. The view is magnificent, the imagery breathtaking, the experience exhilarating. This vision of heaven is the heart of the book! We are being prepared for what is about to follow with seals and trumpets, beasts and bowls.

Chapter 4 focuses on God, the Creator.

Chapter 5 centers on Christ, the Redeemer.

God, the Creator

After this I looked, and there before me was a door standing open in heaven. And the voice I had first heard speaking to me like a trumpet said, "Come up here, and I will show you what must take place after this." At once I was in the Spirit...(4:1,2).

A change of location—from earth to heaven. This is not a geographic or physiological change, but rather a spiritual one. And it is not a future vision. We are invited to see the Lord who is presently being worshiped by the host of heaven!

John is not the first to have an experience of this nature. Some Old Testament prophets, notably Ezekiel, recorded similar visions. And the apostle Paul spoke of being caught up to the "third heaven" (2 Cor. 12:2). Paul was forbidden to reveal what he saw. But no such restriction is placed on John.

While looking through the door in heaven, John experiences the presence of God. "I was in the Spirit." He has a genuine, spiritual experience of God.

Then, through John's description, we enter quietly and gaze in awe at the worship of God and Jesus Christ. The open door allows us to take a peek:

There before me was a throne in heaven with some-one sitting on it (4:2).

The throne is not empty. Someone is seated on the throne. This is the reality! There is a throne in the universe, and the Lord is on that throne. Seventeen times in these two chapters and forty times in the entire book we read about "the throne." The throne of God is the center of the universe. God, the Sovereign Lord, governs the planets and galaxies! God is in supreme command.

He who rules above is also Sovereign below. That was the word of truth to first-century Christians who were suffering awful persecution in the Roman empire. And this is God's message to all believers: God is on His throne. He is in command right now!

*And the one who sat there had the appearance of
jasper and carnelian. A rainbow, resembling an
emerald, encircled the throne (4:3).*

Physically speaking, of course, there are no precious stones in heaven. It is the appearance, the like-
ness we perceive.

Jasper, clear and sparkling like a diamond.

Carnelian, red as a ruby.

Emerald, a quiet deep green that has led some
interpreters to liken it to the divine mercy.

The appearance of a rainbow signals promise. The
rainbow was God's sign to Noah after the flood, testi-
fying that there would never again be a flood to
drown the earth. Now the rainbow encircles the
throne of God—no longer a bow, or half-circle, but
fully round. The full circle may indicate that Jesus
Christ fully accomplished the atonement on the Cross.
This is the gospel—the promises of God are complete,
fulfilled.

*Surrounding the throne were twenty-four other
thrones, and seated on them were twenty-four elders.
They were dressed in white and had crowns of gold
on their heads (4:4).*

The elders are on thrones, too. They have authority
to reign. They represent us: He "has made us to be a
kingdom and priests" (Rev. 1:6). The thrones seem to
be more symbolic than useful, however, for every
time we see the elders, they are not ruling, but falling
down to worship. They are constantly praising God!

They are dressed in white, which symbolizes purity. How their robes became white is explained later
(Rev. 7:14).

Crowns of gold express righteousness that has been tested (as gold is refined by fire) and the authority to reign (crown).

But who are these elders? And why twenty-four? The two most often advanced views are:

(1) *Some identify the elders as angelic beings.* But angels are depicted in Revelation 5:11 as encircling the elders. Angels do not wear crowns, nor do they sing the song of the redeemed. This is not a likely interpretation.

(2) *Others identify the elders as the saints of the Church.* They are the saints of all ages, glorified, and representing all believers before the throne of God.

Why twenty-four? Some think that twenty-four symbolizes the twelve tribes of Israel plus the twelve apostles (12 + 12 = 24). The total number, therefore, would represent both Old and New Testament believers. The entire Church, of course, is not yet in heaven. This is a representative group.

> *From the throne came flashes of lightning, rumblings and peals of thunder. Before the throne, seven lamps were blazing. These are the seven spirits of God. Also before the throne there was what looked like a sea of glass, clear as crystal (4:5,6).*

Here we see the majesty, power and the glory of God. The God whom we serve is awesome. He commands the elements—lightning and thunder. However, the elders do not appear disturbed because of the displays of mighty power. Therefore, we need not be afraid either. We can trust the sovereign Lord who controls the universe!

We are told that the seven lamps represent "the

seven spirits of God." But these are not seven different spirits, but the one Holy Spirit. Possibly, John used
this plural designation in writing to the seven
Churches to emphasize that there is "a Spirit," yet one
and the same, for each church!

The sea of glass heightens the majesty of the One
who sits upon the throne. The sea of glass suggests
that God is holy, separate.

> *In the center, around the throne, were four living
> creatures, and they were covered with eyes, in front
> and in back. The first living creature was like a lion,
> the second was like an ox, the third had a face like a
> man, the fourth was like a flying eagle. Each of the
> four living creatures had six wings and was covered
> with eyes all around, even under his wings. Day
> and night they never stop saying:*

> *"Holy, holy, holy*
> *is the Lord God Almighty*
> *who was, and is, and is to come" (4:6-8).*

These four living creatures are neither human
beings nor angels, since they are mentioned separately from both. Could they be the creatures described in
Ezekiel 1:5-14 and identified as cherubim in Ezekiel
10:20? In Isaiah's vision of God's throne, similar
beings are called seraphim (Isa. 6:2). No one knows
for sure: One writer lists twenty-one possibilities for
solving the mystery of these heavenly beings, finds all
these answers unacceptable and adds number twen-
ty-two, equally unacceptable to most commentators!

Whatever these creatures are, they are vividly
depicted:

One is like a lion, the epitome of strength.

A second is like an ox, a symbol of service.

Still another is like an eagle, representative of swiftness.

And the fourth is like a human being, the crown of God's creation.

They have six wings each. They move well, quickly. They have eyes all around. They don't miss a thing.

And all four of the living creatures join in the general adoration of God.

Why are we accorded this revelation concerning living creatures and elders? Their presence underlines the importance of worshiping God. In heaven, adoration of God is a present reality!

This is the message to the Church: The sovereign Lord is adored in heaven. Ought not the Church on earth to join the heavenly throng in praise and thanksgiving?

> *Whenever the living creatures give glory, honor and thanks to him who sits on the throne and who lives for ever and ever, the twenty-four elders fall down before him who sits on the throne, and worship Him who lives for ever and ever. They lay their crowns before the throne and say:*
>
> *"You are worthy, our Lord and God,*
> *   to receive glory and honor and power,*
> *for you created all things,*
> *   and by your will they were created*
> *   and have their being" (4:9-11)*

The throne is not set in a palace for opulence or splendor, but in the vast spaces of heaven. All praise is accorded the Creator for the splendor of His creation.

The elders lay their crowns before the throne. They humble themselves. They acknowledge that their authority is a *given* authority. They admit that their crowns are tokens which they have not earned, and they return those crowns as an expression of their devotion!

Christ, the Redeemer

> *Then I saw in the right hand of him who sat on the throne a scroll with writing on both sides and sealed with seven seals (5:1).*

The vision continues with a scroll in the hand of God. In the first century, a scroll represented communication. We might have seen a book, a film, or a computer.

The scroll has writing on *both* sides. That is unusual. A scroll generally had writing on one side and was then rolled up with the words inside. Why is the scroll so overwritten? Does this indicate there will be an abundance of judgment?

The scroll is sealed with seven seals. Why seven? One would have been enough! Under Roman law a will had seven seals, documented by seven witnesses. In addition, in the book of Revelation, seven is a symbolic number, denoting perfection. The scroll is *perfectly* sealed. The time for unraveling the specific meaning of the seals will come when they are broken.

> *And I saw a mighty angel proclaiming in a loud voice, "Who is worthy to break the seals and open*

the scroll?" But no one in heaven or on earth or under the earth could open the scroll or even look inside it. I wept and wept because no one was found who was worthy to open the scroll or look inside. Then one of the elders said to me, "Do not weep! See, the Lion of the tribe of Judah, the Root of David, has triumphed. He is able to open the scroll and its seven seals" (5:2-5).

If the scroll remains sealed, the purposes of God will not be carried out. When the scroll is opened, the wrath of God will be poured out on the world, but that is also the time when the redemption of the Church will be completed.

Who is able to open the scroll? One who has the strength for it? One who has the power or the know-how? Apparently, neither strength nor wisdom are qualifications. The question is, who is worthy? Who is without sin? Who has triumphed over the world, the flesh and the devil? Who has won the victory?

No one on earth is worthy: "All have sinned and fall short of the glory of God" (Rom. 3:23). Neither is anyone "under the earth," that is, in Hades, the realm of the dead, able to open the seals. Nor are any creatures in heaven found worthy, for angels have not endured and triumphed over the temptations of the flesh, suffering and death. John could not help but weep at this dilemma, but he stopped crying when he heard that the destiny of the people of God was in safe hands!

Here we have an unforgettable depiction of the inability of humankind and the ability of Jesus Christ, the Son of man, the Son of God, the victorious Lord.

But Jesus is not named. From this point on in

Revelation, Jesus Christ is referred to in symbolic language: "The Lion of the tribe of Judah, the Root of David."

Christians understand these symbols, of course; they resonate with meaning and power. In the Old Testament, the Messiah is identified as the Lion of the tribe of Judah (see Gen. 49:9,10). As the lion is the king of beasts, so Jesus is King of kings. The prophets refer to "a Branch" which will sprout from the kingly line of David (Isa. 11:1).

But for the first-century Christians, the rich and vivid imagery served a practical purpose as well as an expressive one. The hostile Romans would consider this book subversive if it stated outright that Jesus Christ is Emperor, Lord, God and King. All these titles belonged exclusively to Caesar. "The Lion of the tribe of Judah" on the other hand would hardly seem like a threat to the Romans.

Then I saw a Lamb, looking as if it had been slain, standing in the center of the throne, encircled by the four living creatures and the elders. He had seven horns and seven eyes, which are the seven spirits of God sent out into all the earth (5:6).

Instead of a Lion, we now see a Lamb. Twenty-eight times in the book of Revelation, Jesus Christ is referred to as "the Lamb."

Christians comprehend this symbolism also. We know Scripture announces that Jesus Christ is "the Lamb of God, who takes away the sin of the world" (John 1:29). To the Romans, the image of the Lamb must have been even more of a mystery than the concept of the Lion. (A lamb on a throne? How strange!)

The Lamb still shows the marks of crucifixion. We are constantly reminded of the indescribable sacrifice for our sins! Even in eternity, the marks of suffering remain visible on our Lord.

The Lamb is standing, not seated. Elsewhere in the Bible, when the accomplishments of Jesus are summarized, He is pictured as finishing His work and sitting down at the right hand of the Father (see Heb. 1:3). But here, the Lamb stands in the center of the throne. Why? The Lamb is "the center of attention." He stands because He is about to act. The judgment will begin.

"He had seven horns and seven eyes." Do not attempt to visualize a lamb with seven horns and seven eyes; such a picture approaches the weird and eccentric. Jesus did not *actually* have seven horns or eyes. Rather, the number seven stands for completion, perfection. Horns represent power, kingship. Eyes see everything and speak of intelligence. This symbolism means that Jesus has complete authority, power and wisdom to rule.

John himself helps us to understand the horns and eyes. He says that they signify "the Spirit of God." The meaning will become clear—that Jesus will open the seals of judgment in the power of the Spirit.

> *He came and took the scroll from the right hand of him who sat on the throne. And when he had taken it, the four living creatures and the twenty-four elders fell down before the Lamb. Each one had a harp and they were holding golden bowls full of incense, which are the prayers of the saints. (5:7,8)*

The creatures and elders who worshiped God now

join in the adoration of the Lamb. The elders play harps, instruments of song and praise, which help to express their joy. In their hands they hold bowls of incense. The incense represents the prayers of the saints. As incense rises, producing a pleasing aroma, so do the prayers of adoration and thanksgiving, and possibly of intercession, which the Church raises in times of persecution.

The song they sing is *new*. The earlier theme we heard was all about creation (4:11). Now we eavesdrop on the song of redemption:

> *And they sang a new song:*
>
> *"You are worthy to take the scroll*
> *   and to open its seals,*
> *   because you were slain,*
> *   and with your blood you purchased men*
> *   for God*
> *   from every tribe and language and people*
> *   and nation.*
> *You have made them to be a kingdom and priests*
> *   to serve our God,*
> *   and they will reign on the earth" (5:9,10).*

The song is new in time, as the new covenant supersedes the old. The song is also new in quality, from creation to redemption, and it is better than the old song: "The law was given through Moses; grace and truth came through Jesus Christ" (John 1:17). Our redemption was obtained on the Cross. Our redemption will be complete when the Church joins the Lamb in heaven—after the seals are broken.

Salvation purchased by Jesus Christ is not only for a chosen few. God's promise extends to people from every tribe and every nation. The hope of the gospel is universal, not sectarian. The Church is purchased to become kings who reign and priests who serve. John keeps underlining this truth for all Christians in order that we may not lose the vision!

Some insist that our reign with Christ will take place during the Millennium, the thousand years during which Satan will be bound in the abyss (Rev. 20:1). Others construe this authority as a general promise—we will share with Jesus in His Kingdom.

It is important to remind ourselves at this point that the language is symbolic. The Lord has promised that we will participate in His Kingdom. That is all we need to understand at this time. The message is: "Trust in the sovereign God *now*, as you face your enemy in the world. You belong to the Lord and His Kingdom."

> *Then I looked and heard the voice of many angels, numbering thousands upon thousands, and ten thousand times ten thousand. They encircled the throne and the living creatures and the elders. In a loud voice they sang:*
>
> *"Worthy is the Lamb, who was slain, to receive power and wealth and wisdom and strength and honor and glory and praise!"*
>
> *Then I heard every creature in heaven and on earth and under the earth and on the sea, and all that is in them, singing:*

"To him who sits on the throne and to the Lamb
be praise and honor and glory and power
for ever and ever!"

The four living creatures said, "Amen," and the
elders fell down and worshiped (5:11-14).

"Ten thousand times ten thousand": 10,000 x 10,000
= 100,000,000. Did John count the angels? Certainly
not! How could he? The numbers are beyond human
comprehension. The *New English Bible* translation
speaks of "myriads and myriads"—the vast innumerable host of heaven who join in the worship of the
Creator and the Redeemer. The universe itself is joyous with the new song, the song of redemption:
"Worthy is the Lamb, who was slain." He is victorious! He is alive forever more!

Every creature in the universe joins in praise and
adoration. In heaven. On earth. Under the earth. On
the sea. In the sea. In heaven's vision we see the
fulfillment of the promise:

At the name of Jesus every knee should bow,
in heaven and on earth and under the earth,
and every tongue confess that Jesus Christ is Lord
to the glory of God the Father (Phil. 2:10,11).

The Lord who humbled Himself and endured the
cross is now exalted.

The host of heaven acknowledges that the universe
is in the hands of God, the Creator, and theLord Jesus,
our Savior.

Anyone who fails to join in that praise will be left out.

Anyone who cannot sing the new song will have no song to sing.

"Amen" ("So be it!") shout the living creatures."Amen" affirm the elders, as they fall down to worship.

This is the first act of the heavenly play. The drama will continue as the Lamb opens the seven-sealed scroll.

Questions for Discussion and Meditation

1. What would happen if the Church regularly meditated on this vision? What if you did?

2. What new insight do you receive from Revelation 4 and 5 about:

   (a) God, the Father?

   (b) Jesus, the Son?

   (c) heaven?

3. How does the action of the twenty-four elders influence you?

4. If the song of redemption is new, how can it remain new and fresh for you? Do you find answers to that question in this description of heaven?

CHAPTER FOUR

The Seven Seals

Revelation 6

> *Then I watched as the Lamb broke the first of the seven seals (6:1, NEB).*

Here it comes! The seals are opened, and all that is written in and on the scroll comes to pass. God is in control of all these events. He allows the seals to be broken at the proper time, so that His will is accomplished on the earth.

The Four Horsemen of the Apocalypse

> *And I heard one of the four living creatures say in a voice like thunder, "Come!" And there before my eyes was a white horse, and its rider held a bow. He was given a crown, and he rode forth, conquering and to conquer (6:1,2, NEB).*

The operation begins. One of the living creatures announces the first rider. We now understand the function of the four living creatures. They worship the Lord, and they participate in the action. They call forth the horsemen of the Apocalypse.

We forget about the scroll itself as the four horsemen parade before our eyes. In the middle East, horses were rare and special—hardly as abundant as sheep, goats, donkeys or even camels. Rulers rode horses, and conquering nations like the Romans advanced on horseback. People showed respect for horses and stood in awe of them.

The first rider arrives on a white horse. He wears a crown. This description has led some commentators to identify this equestrian as Christ. Who else, they ask, would parade on a white horse and wear a crown? But this interpretation is not in harmony with the horsemen who follow. The other three horsemen are bent on destruction.

Furthermore, it is Jesus Christ as the Lamb who opens the seals. To view the rider on the white horse as Jesus Christ is to confuse the images, since the Lamb continues to release the seals.

Later in the book of Revelation (19:11), *another* white horse appears. The Rider who comes then is called "Faithful and True" and "the Word of God." He is proclaimed as King of king and Lord of lords. There can be no doubt that this second rider of a white horse is Christ. His appearance ends the time of tribulation.

Is the first rider, then, the Antichrist, the long-predicted opponent of Jesus who falsely claims the attributes of Christ (see 1 John 2:18-19)? Does the Antichrist imitate Christ by riding a white horse? Other commentators on Revelation affirm this. But I believe such an interpretation is also farfetched. The Antichrist appears later in the book of Revelation.

Why should he arrive on the scene both here and there?

What confusion! The white horse and its rider have been interpreted as both Christ and Antichrist. How is this possible? The Pharisees were also confused. They accused Jesus of being in league with the devil, of doing His works by the power of Satan.

Another meaning seems closer to the context. The rider on the horse of white, the color of peace (doves, white flags), rides forth "conquering." He stands for peace but holds a bow. A bow and arrows would describe ancient warfare. We may translate these as modern weapons. This rider aims to conquer the world, although he seems to come peacefully.

While the world is deceived by a false peace, disaster strikes! "While people are saying, `Peace and safety,' destruction will come ... suddenly" (1 Thess. 5:3).

The crown which the rider wears is symbolic, too. It simply signifies human authority and rule.

> When the Lamb broke the second seal, I heard the second creature say, "Come!" And out came another horse, all red. To its rider was given power to take peace from the earth and make men slaughter one another; and he was given a great sword (6:3,4, NEB).

The picture is now clear. No more peace on earth—not even false peace. Whatever peace prevailed was short-lived. This rider signals war.

This horse is red, the color of blood. The implication is that blood is spilled throughout the world as war (World War III?) explodes. People destroy each other relentlessly. The poor and helpless nations are conquered by powerful and dominant nations.

A large sword is given to the second rider. This sword, of course, symbolizes all kinds of weapons. The world has progressed far beyond swords and spears and bows and arrows. In the last half-century, we have even gone beyond guns and tanks and entered the era of heat-seeking missiles and nuclear warheads.

The sword is large. Surely our weapons have turned out to be too excessive for us, too numerous!

> *When he broke the third seal, I heard the third creature say, "Come!" And there, as I looked, was a black horse; and its rider held in his hand a pair of scales. And I heard what sounded like a voice from the midst of the living creatures, which said, "A whole day's wage for a quart of flour, a whole day's wage for three quarts of barley-meal! But spare the olive and the vine" (6:5-6, NEB).*

White, red, and now black. The black horse is explained in terms of scarcity, famine and economic hardship—calamities that follow a bloody war. The scales in the hand of the rider are scales of judgment. Scales are also used for weighing food like wheat or barley, meats or vegetables.

The black rider's meaning is clear: food will be scarce and expensive! It takes an eight hour work day to buy one loaf of bread. The price of wheat and common barley is exorbitant! The famines which we are now witnessing in many parts of the world are an indication of the severity of coming plagues.

The meaning of the rider's instructions to "spare the olive and the vine" is less evident. It is important to remember that, in John's day, olive oil and wine were staples, not luxuries. The Good Samaritan traveling from Jerusalem to Jericho carried both oil and wine with him. When he stopped to help the beaten victim by the side of the road, he gave him oil for his wounds and wine to revive him.

Why is the rider not to touch the olive or the vine? Perhaps this vision implies an uneven distribution of resources—there will be plenty of some commodities, scarcity of others. I don't think it's farfetched to speculate that the continuing supply of "the vine" indicates that people will continue to drink in spite of famine and shortages. Or perhaps an uneven distribution of basic resources indicates a scenario in which some people thrive and others suffer—a "rich get richer" situation.

> *When he broke the fourth seal, I heard the voice of the fourth creature say, "Come!" And there, as I looked, was another horse, sickly pale; and its rider's name was Death, and Hades came close behind. To him was given power over a quarter of the earth, with the right to kill by sword and by famine, by pestilence and wild beasts (6:7,8, NEB).*

White, red, black, pale. Pale means "washed out." Our English word "chlorine," the name for the primary ingredient in certain bleaches, is derived from the Greek word translated as "pale."

The meaning of this horseman is specifically explained. He is named Death! And Hades follows on foot, close behind, because in natural course, for those without Christ, Hades follows death! The power accorded both death and Hades in this vision assures us that all these events are permitted by the Lord, who sits on the throne! Remember, we were told in Revelation 1:18 that He holds the keys of death and Hades.

The release of the four horsemen of the Apocalypse causes disaster in the world. Each rider brings more serious consequences than the one before him. The picture is gruesome. People die because of war and famine, because of plague and sickness, and some because of the feared wild beasts which roam freely in certain parts of the earth. An epidemic of fear reigns all over the globe.

One-fourth of the world's population dies! Should we interpret this literally? Numbers in the book of Revelation most likely are not meant to be taken literally, but they *are* important. A "quarter," or a fourth, expresses a significant amount, but also a limited number. The plagues which are yet to come will be greater in their intensity. When the trumpets are sounded, one third of the population will be destroyed (see Rev. 8,9). Then, after the trumpets, the bowls finish off everything (see Rev. 16)!

This is the progression: one-fourth, one-third, total. But again, I don't believe it is necessary to take the numbers literally. What the book of Revelation describes is that the judgments will get progressively worse!

The fifth Seal

> *When he broke the fifth seal, I saw underneath the altar the souls of those who had been slaughtered for God's word and for the testimony they bore (6:9, NEB).*

Relief! The fifth seal is of a different nature. Our attention is drawn to the slain martyrs, to the saints who have died for the Lord.

But this picture raises some questions. How did John "see souls"? Do these souls have form, or are they disembodied? How can you see a soul without a body? And how can a soul be clothed with a white robe, anyway? (6:11) "Souls" do not require robes.

These souls reside under the altar. Is there an altar in heaven? A temple? According to Revelation 21:22, there is no temple in the New Jerusalem. If there is no temple, there can be no altar.

The prophet must be speaking figuratively. The souls and the altar are part of the rich imagery of the vision. "The Lord is in his holy temple," cries out the prophet Habakkuk (2:20). The message is that the martyrs have survived death, and that they are now with God—yes, close to the altar which signifies the sacrifice of Jesus Christ. They trusted in Jesus Christ, kept the word of God and remained faithful. Their martyrdom was not in vain.

In the letters to the seven churches (Rev. 2–3), the Lord emphasized the importance of maintaining faith in Jesus Christ. Christians were exhorted to hold fast and to persevere. Now we see evidence that the martyrs who retain their testimony to the end are rewarded!

This is a word of comfort for the Church. Death is not the end. After death, the souls of those who die in Christ are protected under the altar of God! Therefore Christians need not be anxious or afraid. We can live by faith in the Lamb of God. The Lord is with us. Eternal life is His gift to us.

They called out in a loud voice, "How long, Sovereign Lord, holy and true, until you judge the inhabitants of the earth and avenge our blood?" (6:10).

That is the fervent prayer of the Church during times of persecution! How long will this trial persist? How long will You allow the world to persecute Your people? How long will You provide the forces of evil with the power to put us to death? Lord, do You care? Where is Your power? You are sovereign, so why don't You put a stop to this suffering?

Revelation assured us that God is on the throne of the universe! Why, then, this delay? What is required to bring justice to the world? What is the holdup? The question hangs in the air.

This prayer of the Church also seems to contain a cry for vengeance. Is that a Christian prayer? How can the Church pray for vengeance if we believe in forgiveness?

But look at it again: "How long, Sovereign Lord ...until you judge..." This prayer is not for vengeance, but for God's justice. The saints are asking God to effect righteous judgment, to set things straight! They are not calling for a personal vendetta. Rather, they are asking: How long, O Lord, until You accomplish Your will on earth as it is done in heaven?

The necessity of justice is a basic theme in Scripture. Abel's blood cries out for justice. The prophets affirm that God will usher in a reign of righteousness and truth. All wrongs must be righted. The final judgment is in the hands of the Sovereign Lord. We are assured that justice will prevail and that the sacrifices of the martyrs has not been in vain.

When will the prayer of the Church be answered? That is the question:

Then each of them was given a white robe, and they were told to wait a little longer, until the number of their fellow servants and brothers who were to be killed as they had been was completed (6:11).

The Lord will come soon. The wait is only a little longer.

But there is an "until"—they are to wait until the number of their fellow martyrs is completed. This means still more Christians will be killed! Why? Why more suffering? Why is the world allowed to pursue its wicked and evil devices?

This is one of those unanswerable questions. Who knows why evil has such a long day? We do not know; only the Lord knows the reason. But the word of the living God assures us that there will be an end to it all. Believing in the Lord who brings that final judgment, we are encouraged to hold on just a little longer. There is never a good reason to repudiate our faith!

While they wait, the martyrs receive white robes to cover their unworthiness. They are pronounced worthy by the righteousness of Christ. All spots are washed out; they are white, clean.

Then I watched as he broke the sixth seal. And there was a violent earthquake; the sun turned black as a funeral pall and the moon all red as blood; and the stars in the sky fell to earth, like figs shaken down by

a gale; the sky vanished, as a scroll is rolled up, and
every mountain and island was moved from its place
(6:12-14, NEB).

Everywhere there is havoc, terror, fear!

An earthquake rolls through the earth. The foundations are shaken.

The sun turns black—a frightening sight. What shall we make of it? No more light or heat? No more life on earth?

The moon is red. We stare at the night sky and cannot figure it out. Our vision is dimmed.

The stars fall to earth? How can that be? Most stars would destroy the earth, since many stars and planets are larger than the earth. What John describes are the terrors of judgment day!

The sky rolled up like a scroll? What will that look like? Can we perceive it? What will we *see* if there is no sky?

Every mountain and island moved from its place. Where to? Are they cast into the sea?

If we interpret this seal literally, we face the unthinkable—the total destruction of the earth, the snuffing out of all forms of life. What, then, of the rest of the book of Revelation? The book continues, the end is not yet come!

It seems clear, therefore, that we need to interpret this part of the vision symbolically. We are viewing a dramatic picture of events which describe the most horrible things imaginable. Signs in the heavens—the sun, moon, stars and even the sky itself—and on earth, mountains and islands dislodged.

The earth beneath us rumbles, the foundations are

shaken, the roof disappears, solids liquefy, terror reigns. All security vanishes.

> *Then the kings of the earth, the princes, the generals, the rich, the mighty, and every slave and every free man hid in caves and among the rocks of the mountains. They called to the mountains and the rocks, "Fall on us and hide us from the face of him who sits on the throne and from the wrath of the Lamb! For the great day of their wrath has come, and who can stand?" (6:15-17)*

From top to bottom, from kings to slaves, every stratum of society is obsessed with fear and panic. The strong will not be able to deliver the strong. The powerful will be powerless. Alarm takes hold of the government, the economy, the military, and all who live without God.

It is not that people lack an awareness of God. The Creator has revealed Himself in creation, and the world has heard about Jesus. People have been vaguely aware of a coming judgment: "The great day of their wrath has come!" And now they are aware that judgment is taking place.

The world's reaction to judgment is understandable. People are gripped by fear. They even wish for death, and they try to flee. And yet there is no repentance! No matter how severe the judgment of God becomes, their hearts remain hardened.

This is a message for the Church. We are told to look at reality, at the way things really are around us! The secular society will not be saved. The world will not be converted, because they are not about to repent. In view of that hard truth, Christians are to persist in the faith!

People stream to the mountains. They want the rocks to fall on them. To die would be better than this judgment, so the world reasons.

How can the mountains and rocks hide anyone from God? Is God blocked out by their mass? Of course not. There is no hiding place. The world must face the Judge! Adam and Eve were the first to hide from the presence of the Lord. Now the whole world is confounded and afraid!

Six seals have been opened. Before we observe the peeling of the seventh seal, we will hear another word of comfort, a word to help the church to persevere.

Questions for Discussion and Meditation

1. What is the purpose of the seven seals?

2. How does the world react to the judgment of God?

3. What is the message of the seals for Christians, then and now?

4. What difference does the coming judgment make for your life today?

CHAPTER FIVE

The 144,000

Revelation 7

We get a breather before the seventh and last seal is opened. Something very important is interjected before the drama continues. This same pattern occurs after the six trumpets, before the seventh. There is a structure as well as a purpose to the book of Revelation.

What is the reason for this interlude? A message of utmost significance for all Christians!

> *After this I saw four angels stationed at the four corners of the earth, holding back the four winds so that no wind should blow on sea or land or on any tree. Then I saw another angel rising out of the east, carrying the seal of the living God; and he called aloud to the four angels who had been given power to ravage land and the sea: "Do no damage to sea or land or trees until we have set the seal of our God upon the foreheads of his servants"* (7:1-3, NEB).

Even though the earth seemed to be falling apart in chapter 6, nature is not out of control. The angels of God are in charge of the elements. And they are now commissioned to hold back the winds that rage from every direction! The purpose of this action is to keep the earth from destruction. If a hurricane is unleashed, everything could be wrecked and broken. The angels prevent the winds of judgment from howling on creation—for now.

The trees in this passage represent the living things of nature. Trees and other living things are certainly vulnerable when fierce winds roar!

The four angels are pictured as standing at the four corners of the earth. This does not imply that the earth is square. (*Neither* can we conclude that the Bible writers knew the earth is round!) "The four corners of the earth" is a figure of speech. It refers to our experience of the four directions—north, south, east and west—from whence winds seem to arise.

(We, too, normally talk about nature as we experience it, not necessarily according to our scientific understanding. We say, for example, "Did you see the sunrise this morning?" or "Did you see the sunset?" when we know perfectly well that the earth rotated on its axis and the sun didn't move!)

The fifth angel is commissioned by God to reinforce God's protection on the earth. Until the servants of God are "sealed," no harm will come upon the earth on land or sea.

The seal means protection, but it also marks ownership. We have been redeemed by Jesus Christ. We belong to Him. Ownership includes protection. The seal is probably not an actual, visible insignia. It is a spiritual mark—a sealing of the heart.

The 144,000

*Then I heard the number of those who were sealed:
144,000 from all the tribes of Israel.*

*From the tribe of Judah 12,000 were sealed,
from the tribe of Reuben 12,000,
from the tribe of Gad 12,000,
from the tribe of Asher 12,000,
from the tribe of Naphtali 12,000,
from the tribe of Manasseh 12,000,
from the tribe of Simeon 12,000,
from the tribe of Levi 12,000,
from the tribe of Issachar 12,000
from the tribe of Zebulon 12,000,
from the tribe of Joseph 12,000,
from the tribe of Benjamin 12,000 (7:4-8).*

This precise summation sounds as if we are dealing strictly with 144,000 specific individuals. As described here, they are all Jews, chosen from the twelve tribes of Israel, with the same exact number taken from each tribe.

If we adopt a literal view of Revelation, as some commentators do, we cannot escape that interpretation. And indeed, some people believe there will be 144,00 Jewish converts that serve as missionaries during the time of tribulation.

But this interpretation raises several problems. In the first place, there is a slight variation of the original twelve tribes. Dan is missing, Manasseh is included. So the effort to force the 144,000 onto the original 12 tribes of Israel fails. Why was the tribe of Dan omitted? Because of the idols set up in the northern kingdom? Some commentators project the Antichrist to proceed from the tribe of Dan. Pure conjecture!

A more important issue arises from looking at the book of Revelation as a whole. True, the 144,000 are said here to be culled from the tribes of Israel. But they are also called "servants of our God" (v. 3), and whenever Revelation mentions "servants of God" in other chapters, it does so without any racial reference (see Rev. 2:20; 19:2,5; 22:3,6). Furthermore, in Revelation 14, we read again about the 144,000, and this time they are not identified as coming from the twelve tribes of Israel. So can we unequivocally state that this number will be equally divided among the Jewish tribes?

It is important to remember that apocalyptic literature tends to be full of details. We can see this in other books of the Bible such as Daniel and Ezekiel and in the Apocrypha (the books between the Old and New Testament). That, most likely, is why the number 144,000 is broken down into twelve specific tribes, a detail which seems unnecessary and superfluous to us. As far as apocalyptic literature is concerned, it is not strange at all.

The point is that with some prophetic books it is *not expected* that we hold to a literal interpretation of the text! Details were not supposed to be analyzed; their purpose was to intensify the effect.

The Israel of God

Still, the number 144,000 must signify something. What? Some scholars point out that we arrive at 144,000 by multiplying twelve times twelve by one thousand: 12 x 12 x 1000 = 144,000. One twelve could designate the apostles, the other twelve the tribes of Israel listed in the passage. And in Jewish thought, one thousand (like other multiples of ten) is considered a perfect number. Therefore, 12 x 12 x 1000 could specify Jews (the twelve tribes) and Christians (the twelve apostles), unified and perfected in Jesus Christ.

This interpretation is in line with the teaching of the rest of the New Testament.

Jesus made a promise to the apostles: "You who have followed me will also sit on twelve thrones, judging the twelve tribes of Israel" (Matt. 19:28). On that premise the New Testament pictures the Church as the new Israel.

In Galatians 6:16 Paul sends peace and mercy to "the Israel of God." In view of the context, a majority of scholars hold that "the Israel of God" refers to the *new* Israel, the Church.

James addresses his letter "to the twelve tribes scattered among the nations" (James 1:1). Is he writing to the twelve Jewish tribes or to Christians? Some Christians whom he addresses may be of Jewish origin, but the total context of the letter suggests that in his greeting to the twelve tribes he is saluting the Christian Church! "Twelve tribes" means "Christians"!

What then is the place of Israel in the New Testament? Paul discusses this very subject in Romans 9-11. The hope of redemption for Israel remains! But Paul states unequivocally that God is now working through the Church. This is the same body John addresses in the book of Revelation!

What are we to assume, then? Who are the 144,000? Remember, *the book of Revelation is addressed to the seven churches!* Therefore we cannot conclude that the 144,000 are Jews culled from every tribe. Nor is it necessary to retain the exact number 144,000. That number designates believers of both Old and New Testament times.

We are at liberty to interpret apocalyptic literature in this manner, in fact we must do so, if we are to remain true to the intention of the Apocalypse!

The 144,000 are sealed (7:4). So is the entire Church (9:4). All Christians are prepared for martyrdom. But even in martyrdom as the judgment intensifies, they are to trust in the promises of the Lord.

A Great Multitude—The Redeemed

> *"After this I looked and there before me was a great multitude that no one could count, from every nation, tribe, people and language, standing before the throne and in front of the Lamb. They were wearing white robes and were holding palm branches in their hands. And they cried out in a loud voice:*
>
> *"Salvation belongs to our God,*
> *who sits on the throne,*
> *and to the Lamb." (7:9,10).*

Who is this great multitude? This must be the Church! Such a throng that it cannot be counted. Is this a different group from the 144,000 who have been sealed? If the 144,000 represent the Church, then who is this company? Do we need to reverse our position? Are the 144,000 Jews after all, and this multitude the Christians? *No!* The answer shines through this very passage.

These Christians come from every nation, tribe and people. The vision emphasizes the spread and scope of the gospel, for these Christians represent the redeemed from the entire earth. Seeing this vast throng is an encouragement to those Christians who are about to endure the coming, dark hour!

Jesus announced: "I have other sheep that are not of this sheep pen. I must bring them also. They too will listen to my voice, and there shall be one flock and one shepherd" (John.10:16). This is the vast multitude we now envision in the book of Revelation—the "other sheep." Jewish and Christian believers together will form one flock.

Why then should we distinguish between the 144,000 and the multitude? The redeemed will be without number! God asked Abraham if he could count the grains of sand in the deserts and beaches of the world. So was his seed to be! Those who follow in the steps of faith are the true children of Abraham.

They stand before the throne of the Lamb. They believe in the Lamb of God who takes away the sin of the world. Therefore they are given white robes— purity and righteousness in Christ—and palm branches—which symbolize the joy of victory.

The redeemed celebrate the bliss of salvation. If there is rejoicing in heaven over one sinner who repents, the joy of this vast throng knows no bounds!

All the angels were standing around the throne and around the elders and the four living creatures. They fell down on their faces before the throne and worshiped God, saying,

"Amen!

Praise and glory
and wisdom and thanks and honor
and power and strength
be to our God for ever and ever.
Amen!" (7:11,12).

The worship of God resounds in heaven. No matter what is about to happen on earth, let all Christians join in praise!

Then one of the elders asked me, "These in white
robes—who are they, and where did they come from?
I answered, "Sir, you know." And he said, "These
are they who have come out of the great tribulation;
they have washed their robes and made them white
in the blood of the Lamb (7:13,14).

The innumerable throng overwhelms John. He does not know where they come from until the answer is revealed to him: They come out of the great tribulation. And then he is told how their robes became white: They have been washed in the blood of the Lamb!

As anyone knows who has ever attempted to do laundry, you cannot get clothes clean by washing them in blood. Surely no one will dispute that we are dealing with symbolism and not literalism here!

Then why must we force a literal interpretation on the words "the great tribulation"? Is there to be a special, final period of trial at the end of the age? Some teach that "the great tribulation" will last seven years, some that it will take only three and a half years. They get these precise figures from books which are not meant to be taken precisely!

Is it permissible to interpret this reference as *the tribulation the church has always endured at the hands of Satan?*

These are the words of Jesus: "Those will be days of distress unequaled from the beginning, when God created the world, until now—and never to be equaled again" (Mark 13:19). From the context it is evident that Jesus was speaking about the destruction of Jerusalem in A.D. 70: "Let those who are in Judea flee to the mountains." (Mark 13:14) However, these words have also been applied to the end times. They can refer to A.D. 70 *and* a great tribulation during the last days. What if we understand "the great tribulation" to indicate that this multitude has made it into the presence of God and the Lamb *through persecution and suffering over the course of history,* even though there could still be a special time of tribulation at the end? Then the book of Revelation is written for Christians in every age and in every place—all those who endure the assault of the world, the flesh and the devil.

We need not water down the terrible times which are prophesied for the end. There will be "great tribulation"; Jesus said so. There has also been tribulation from the beginning of the Christian movement. And the main point of this chapter is that the innumerable throng which John sees before the throne have endured it! They are now secure, delivered, completed. The most awful persecution has failed to stop the triumphant procession of the redeemed.

The book of Revelation is not a story of dissolution and decay, but of hope and promise. The redeemed come out of the world rejoicing and praising God!

This is the message for Christians at all times and in

all places! Revelation may have more scenes of horror than any other New Testament book, but it also provides hope and continual reassurance. Revelation is a book of comfort and promise—the promise of eternal life with God.

Therefore,

> *"they are before the throne of God*
>   *and serve him day and night in his temple;*
> *and he who sits on the throne will spread his*
>   *tent over them.*
> *Never again will they hunger;*
>   *never again will they thirst.*
> *The sun will not beat upon them,*
>   *nor any scorching heat.*
> *For the Lamb at the center of the throne will*
>   *betheir shepherd;*
> *he will lead them to springs of living water*
> *And God will wipe away every tear from*
>   *their eyes" (7:15-17).*

In this eloquent picture of joy and comfort in God's presence, the worship of God continues day and night. Service is not for an eight-hour day; it is continual.

The tent of God implies security, protection. There is nothing to be afraid of in God's service!

Neither is there any bodily need—not hunger or thirst. We will be satisfied with the Bread of Life and the Living Water—Jesus Christ.

The sun can be scorching in the desert. For people who know what it is like to live in the desert, to be delivered from the burning sun is a comforting word.

And now we come to a beautiful shift in imagery. Jesus the Lamb is now referred to as the Shepherd. So the Lamb who was slain becomes our Shepherd! He laid down His life for us. Now He protects us and leads us by the still waters.

In heaven all tears will be wiped away. In the final chapters of the book of Revelation we read in more detail of the joy of eternity. For the present we are accorded a preview. For those who follow Christ, there will come a time of no more sorrow, no more tears, no more death.

Questions for Discussion and Meditation

1. What is the message of chapter 7 for Christians today?

2. How does this vision help us to face whatever the future may bring?

3. What are the promises of God for the faithful? What is our hope?

CHAPTER SIX

The Seven Trumpets

Revelation 8 and 9

*When he opened the seventh seal, there was silence
in heaven for about half an hour (8:1).*

Silence in heaven! A time of prayer and medita-
tion? The praise of God and the singing of songs ceas-
es—the quiet before the storm!

John writes about a "half-hour" of silence. He must
be measuring in human terms. How can there be "a
half-hour" in heaven? Who keeps time in eternity?

Why this silence? Because of the serious scene we
have just witnessed? Because of the suffering saints
who have endured the horrors of history? Because of
the coming judgment—the plagues about to scourge
the earth? Or does God silence the angels in order to
listen to the prayers of the saints?

Whatever the answer, here is a dramatic pause
before the trumpets blow!

*And I saw the seven angels who stand before God,
and to them were given seven trumpets. Another*

angel, who had a golden censer, came and stood at the altar. He was given much incense to offer, with the prayers of all the saints, on the golden altar before the throne. The smoke of the incense, together with the prayers of the saints, went up before God from the angel's hand. Then the angel took the censer, filled it with fire from the altar, and hurled it on the earth; and there came peals of thunder, rumblings, flashes of lightning and an earthquake (8:2-5).

Who are these seven angels before the throne? Their task is to blow seven trumpets, a complete round. (Throughout Revelation, seven stands for the perfect number.) But before they blast, another angel appears. His task seems to be to make sure the prayers of the saints are heard and *answered!*

The response of heaven is symbolized by fire from the altar which is returned to earth, turning into thunder and lightning, earthquakes and rumblings. This is how God answers the prayers of the Church. The prayers of the saints witness to the power of God And while the Church prays, the judgment falls!

The First Trumpet

In Old Testament times, trumpets summoned Israel to worship, to the celebration of feasts, and to war. They also sounded alarms. Trumpets always announced something. These trumpets announce the judgment of God.

Then the seven angels who had the seven trumpets prepared to sound them. The first angel sounded his trumpet, and there came hail and fire mixed with

blood, and it was hurled down upon the earth. A
third of the earth was burned up, a third of the trees
were burned up, and all the green grass was burned
up (8:6,7).

The first four trumpets bring plagues that represent
the judgment of God on nature. Some of these plagues
parallel the plagues that struck Egypt when Moses led
Israel out of slavery.

A hailstorm is bad enough. Adding fire and blood
to the hail turns it into a fearful, unnatural turbulence.
The unknown and unfamiliar rains down from the
sky, and therefore from God. This hailstorm creates a
certain terror for humanity!

The fire burns up a third of the earth. When the
seals were opened, only a fourth of the world was
damaged. Without taking these figures literally, we
realize that the devastation of earth becomes progressively worse—from one-fourth to one-third.

The Second Trumpet

The second angel sounded his trumpet, and some-
thing like a huge mountain, all ablaze, was thrown
into the sea. A third of the sea turned into blood, a
third of the living creatures in the sea died, and a
third of the ships were destroyed (8:8,9).

What happens here involves not an authentic
mountain, but "something like" a mountain. Is this a
volcanic eruption? Does a large object from the sky
fall into the sea? Is the world perhaps facing ther-
monuclear warfare? Or does a powerful nation
(mountain) vanquish many people (sea)? This is pos-

sible; often, in Scripture, mountains represent kingdoms and seas symbolize groups of people. Whatever the exact meaning, it is clear that the language of the Apocalypse describes the judgment of God on the world.

Again a third, a significant part of nature, is stricken—this time the sea and life in the sea. Nevertheless, not all is destroyed. A third indicates a limited and controlled judgment. And yet what a loss to the world's navies and shipping industries!

The Third Trumpet

> *The third angel sounded his trumpet, and a great star, blazing like a torch, fell from the sky on a third of the rivers and on the springs of water—the name of the star is Wormwood. A third of the waters turned bitter, and many people died from the waters that had become bitter (8:10,11).*

A "star" falls from the sky? Is it a meteor? A planet? It is something from the sky, therefore something from God!

The star is named Wormwood, which means "bitter" or "poison." And what the star does is bitter indeed. One third—a limited portion—of the rivers, lakes and reservoirs are poisoned. What happens to the drinking water for millions of people?

Many people die. And yet these phenomena do not produce the sorrow that leads to repentance. We are not notified of anyone who turns to God. How strange! No one seeks the Lord during these perilous times? The signs in the sky remind people that they are but flesh, and yet the world fails to repent of sin.

Human nature is not affected. Human pride is not subdued.

The Fourth Trumpet

The fourth angel sounded his trumpet, and a third of the sun was struck, a third of the moon, and a third of the stars, so that a third of them turned dark. A third of the day was without light, and also a third of the night (8:12).

The repeated emphasis of "a third" is symbolic. How can one-third of the sun become dark? We know that the moon can appear in different shapes, but we must not be swept away by an exact application. The point is that there is terrifying darkness both during the day and at night.

What is the meaning of darkness? Darkness signals the judgment of God. Jesus Christ is the Light of the world, and Christians are to walk in the Light. Outside of Christ, there is only darkness, and those who are not in the Kingdom are condemned to darkness. Outside of heaven, it is dark everywhere!

It is important to note that these last signs occur in the sky above. God is enthroned "above." He is in control of these omens. Even the people of earth understand and admit that these judgments come from God, although they do not repent (Rev.6:16,17)!

As I watched, I heard an eagle that was flying in midair call out in a loud voice: "Woe! Woe! Woe to the inhabitants of the earth, because of the trumpet blasts about to be sounded by the other three angels" (8:13).

Just as we have become used to seeing angels and living creatures and all manner of plagues, why do we have to cope with a talking eagle?

Who knows? Artists take liberties, and John is like a surrealist painter who drapes a melting timepiece over the edge of a table. Even though we may try to explain their art, we can't be certain what they are telling us! Nevertheless, we receive impressions that are more powerful than rational explanations can provide.

The appearance of the eagle does punctuate the difference between the first four trumpets and the next three. The first four trumpets brought judgment that afflicted nature primarily. The next trumpets will directly afflict a rebellious society, and they will be worse than anything the world has experienced so far. Perhaps that's why the eagle appears. His announcement is a kind of prologue.

Three times the eagle cries out "Woe." There are three trumpets to go.

What is the point? This brief interruption before the next trumpets is a serious warning for the earth's inhabitants. Now, whenever John speaks of "inhabitants of the earth," he means people who do not believe in Jesus Christ. His specific wording indicates that the Church will be preserved in spite of these woes. Trouble is the lot of those who refuse to worship God and Jesus Christ.

We can see parallels between the seals and trumpets—and the bowls that will be described in Revelation 16. For example, with the opening of the sixth seal, the sun, moon and stars are affected, and with the blowing of the fourth trumpet, a third of the sun, moon and stars turn dark. The fourth bowl will be poured out on the sun, causing it to scorch people with its fire.

Revelation, like other examples of apocalyptic literature, is not a perfectly organized, chronological work. If we keep this in mind, it is easier to stay aware of a developing story rather than the historical sequence. John's purpose is not to chronicle history. He is telling a story, sharing a vision, and in the process he may repeat himself to intensify some impressions.

The Fifth Trumpet

The fifth angel sounded his trumpet, and I saw a star that had fallen from the sky to the earth. The star was given the key to the shaft of the Abyss. When he opened the Abyss, smoke rose from it like the smoke from a gigantic furnace. The sun and sky were darkened by the smoke from the Abyss (9:1,2).

The metaphors are mixed in this passage. A star falls from the sky and is given a key, which opens the Abyss. Does this star represent an angel? The devil? A person? Certainly the star does not remain an inanimate object.

As in the case of the speaking eagle, it is difficult to be definitive—and it is not necessary. What the star-person *does* is more important to note than who he is.

He has a key which opens the Abyss. Not an actual key, of course. The key is a figure of speech denoting authority. We have already been informed (Rev. 1:18) that Jesus Christ has the keys of death and Hades. This means that He has the authority to open and close the most feared prospects of human existence.

The Abyss itself speaks of the lowest places in hell. It is the bottomless pit, the place where the demons reside. When the Abyss is unlocked, smoke billows forth which is so dense that it even obliterates the sun. What is about to proceed from the unlocked Abyss is horrible!

> *And out of the smoke locusts came down upon the earth and were given power like that of scorpions of the earth. They were told not to harm the grass of the earth or any plant or tree, but only those people who did not have the seal of God on their foreheads. They were not given power to kill them, but only to torture them for five months. And the agony they suffered was like that of the sting of a scorpion when it strikes a man. During those days men will seek death, but will not find it; they will long to die, but death will elude them (9:3-6).*

Locusts were greatly feared in the Middle East in John's day. An infestation of locusts is a dreadful, ravaging, *total* plague that plunders the land, nature, crops. This scourge is on people! The insects destroy everything in their path.

And yet these are no ordinary locusts. (That would have been disturbing enough.) These locusts have the added characteristics of scorpions, another feared pest in the Middle East. The poisonous sting of scorpions is extremely painful, like the sting of a bumblebee that does not abate.

The pests have been given special power, which they are to exercise not on nature, but on people. Not on Christians, though—the Christians have been sealed and are therefore protected from the scourge of locusts. Will the Church escape the curse of the locusts? Will Christians be "stung" or "not stung"? Does the protection from the Lord mean to escape affliction? Possibly. But it could also imply the power to endure affliction through faith.

The torture is to last five months. What does that mean? Why *five* months? A clue may be found in the fact that the life cycle of a locust is five months. The plague lasts as long as the locusts thrive.

The pestilence fills people with appalling dread, which is followed by despair and depression. Those who live without hope of heaven wish for death. Life must be terrible for people who, having no eternal hope, prefer to end it all rather than suffer the pain of a doomed existence!

And how are we to understand the prohibition not to hurt the grass, when during the first trumpet blast all the green grass was burned up? This and similar questions are not germane.

Once again, the book of Revelation is not a precise document. It is not like a puzzle whose pieces were designed to fit neatly together. Sometimes Revelation may not sound logical at all. It is more like an art exhibition than a history lecture. In an art show we often don't see a *logical* sequence of subject matter, although there may well be an *artistic* progression and development. The fact that many questions are left unanswered in Revelation does not take away from its power or significance.

As commentator E. F. Scott remarks, "a perfectly logical apocalypse would be a contradiction in terms."[1]

The locusts looked like horses prepared for battle. On their heads they wore something like crowns of gold, and their faces resembled human faces. Their hair was like women's hair, and their teeth were like lions' teeth. They had breastplates like breastplates of iron, and the sound of their wings was like the thundering of many horses and chariots rushing into battle. They had tails and stings like scorpions, and in their tails they had power to torment people for five months. They had as king over them the angel of the Abyss, whose name in Hebrew is Abaddon, and in Greek, Apollyon. The first woe is past; two other woes are yet to come (9:7-12).

The locusts are still locusts. They only look like horses—horses ready for battle. In other words, they have a look of potency which produces terror. The crowns on their heads represent awesome power.

Worst of all are the human faces on these insect-like creatures! This means they are intelligent! The world will have to cope not with animal, but with human mentality.

The locusts have women's hair, long and flowing. And when they open their mouths, they reveal their most frightening potential. They have the teeth of a lion; they can devour whatever crosses their path.

Breastplates indicate protection. The description of these beasts sounds like something from a science fiction film. But unlike most movie aliens, these creatures cannot be stopped.

Wings denote swiftness. These can quickly escape from any counterattack. And their powerful wings make thunderous noise! There is no getting away from this pandemonium!

Once more we read of the scorpion's sting, which torments people for five months before the wound can heal. What a fantastic description of unnatural cruelty! Pablo Picasso's "Guernica," which graphically depicts the horrors of war, pales beside it!

The locusts are governed and controlled by a king whose name translates as "The Destroyer." This leader materializes from the demonic Abyss.

What does the scourge of locusts mean? An actual invasion of insects or other vermin? A physical pestilence? Helicopters with poisonous gas? Nuclear warfare? Since these locust-scorpions arise from the Abyss, could they represent demon possession? Some interpreters offer wild ideas.

To understand the significance of the locusts, we need to ask what the purpose of this plague is. What do the locusts do? The answer could lie in what follows the invasion of locusts: "men will seek death." We could speculate about a worldwide epidemic of hopelessness and depression, resulting in a rash of suicide attempts which will keep the emergency rooms in hospitals hopping. The engulfing depression could be the product of demonic forces let loose in the world, producing mental as well as physical torture. In fact, the mental may be more severe than the physical. This is the first of three woes.

The Sixth Trumpet

> *The sixth angel sounded his trumpet, and I heard a voice coming from the horns of the golden altar that is before God. It said to the sixth angel who had the trumpet, "Release the four angels who are bound at the great river Euphrates." And the four*

angels who had been kept ready for this very hour
and day and month and year were released to kill a
third of mankind. The number of the mounted
troops was two hundred million. I heard their
number. (9:13-16).

The storm breaks loose at the very hour appointed
by God. Yet again we are reminded that God is in control of history. The angels do His bidding. The world
and its rulers are in His hands. In God's timing, the
world experiences the wrath of God before experienc-
ing His righteousness.

The angels apparently had been holding back a vast
horde of troops at the River Euphrates until this
moment. Now they lead them into battle. The
Euphrates was a natural boundary in biblical days.
Abraham was given the land west of the Euphrates.
The Romans extended their domain to the Euphrates.
And from beyond the Euphrates came the feared
armies of the Eastern nations.

Now, pouring over this natural boundary, is a huge
number of mounted troops—so many that John could
never count them. He *heard* that two hundred million
was their number. Does this mean precisely two hundred million? More likely, the number represents a
vast, innumerable army. They come from the
East—perhaps from China?

This was how I saw the horses and their riders in
my vision: They wore breastplates, fiery red, blue,
and sulphur-yellow; the horses had heads like lions'
heads, and out of their mouths came fire, smoke,
and sulphur. By these three plagues,....a third of

mankind was killed. The power of the horses lay in their mouths, and in their tails also; for their tails were like snakes, with heads, and with them they dealt injuries (9:17-19, NEB).

This army is as terrifying as the hideous locust-scorpions. Their breastplates represent armored protection; apparently, they are unbeatable. Their horses have heads like lions—the most feared of beasts. Out of their mouths issue fire, smoke and sulfur. They are like creatures from the beyond. There is no way to stop the raging fires or escape the sweeping effects of smoke and sulfur.

After these horses have passed by, the worst is yet to come. Their tails sting like cobras. There is no escape from these creatures coming or going!

The result of this invasion is that one third of the human race is destroyed. A large number—yet, once again, a limited number.

Some interpret the results of blowing the sixth trumpet as modern warfare. (It is true that the nations of the world certainly have weapons capable of exterminating millions.) In this scenario, the horses become horsepower, tanks. The mouths that spit fire and the tails that sting are like guns that kill from the front or back of armored equipment. Sulfur is compared to chemical warfare.

Perhaps. But the central point is that God is now judging the world, a world which has consistently opposed, blasphemed, rejected, crucified, and ignored Jesus Christ. The world receives just retribution for its evil deeds. But the result of this tribulation contains a foretaste of doom.

The rest of mankind that were not killed by these plagues still did not repent of the work of their hands; they did not stop worshiping demons, and idols of gold, silver, bronze, stone and wood—idols that cannot see or hear or walk. Nor did they repent of their murders, their magic arts, their sexual immorality or their thefts (9:20,21).

Unbelief is very persistent!

The hearts of people are unchanged. Insufferable, odious plagues have afflicted the earth. War has broken out, killing men and women and children, but the worship of false gods persists! The world continues to serve its homemade idols. People live for pleasure, power, money, and all their self-serving ends. No one turns to the living God on the throne of the universe?

The crime rate spirals upward. The number of murders, thefts, assaults, rapes and robberies does not go down. Sexual transgressions abound; there is no end to adultery and fornication. Human nature dictates the action.

What kind of sins are lumped together! Murder and stealing. Sorcery, magic arts, the occult, devil worship and sexual sins! Anyone of these sins can keep people from accepting and receiving the grace of God.

Repentance is difficult for those whose hearts are hardened. Repentance requires not only humility, but a desire to forsake self-made idols. Repentance means a change in our self-indulgent life. Repentance is only possible when we respond to the revelation of Jesus Christ.

This is why the judgment of God persists. Justice will be done. The holy God will not sweep sin and rebellion under the rug. The sovereign Lord will not overlook brutality against the innocent, crimes against truth and beauty, outrage against love and purity, violence against His only, beloved Son. The righteous God will come forward in judgment when His offer of grace is rejected.

If God did nothing about the sins of the world, He would be a soft-hearted, weak victim. If there were no judgment, then God would not be God.

Questions for Discussion and Meditation

1. What are the consequences of believing in a God of justice and righteousness? What are the consequences for the unjust? For the just?

2. Why is the creation affected by the judgment of God?

3. How much pain and persecution can any person withstand?

4. What is revealed about human nature by these trumpet-judgments?

CHAPTER SEVEN

The Word and the Witnesses

Revelation 10 and 11

Before the seventh trumpet sounds, there is an intermission, just as there was between the sixth and seventh seal. While the seventh trumpet is delayed two questions are answered for us:

(1) How long will it be before the end of the tribulation?

(2) What is the purpose of the Church during this terrible time of testing?

The Angel and the Word

Then I saw another mighty angel coming down from heaven. He was robed in a cloud, with a rainbow above his head; his face was like the sun, and his legs were like fiery pillars. He was holding a little scroll,

*which lay open in his hand. He planted his right foot
on the sea and his left foot on the land, and he gave a
loud shout like the roar of a lion. When he shouted,
the voices of the seven thunders spoke. And when the
seven thunders spoke, I was about to write; but I
heard a voice from heaven say, "Seal up what the
seven thunders have said and do not write it down"*
(10:1-4).

An angel is described as having strength and
might, but how large is he? Is he huge? He is able to
put one foot on the sea and the other on land. If we
take this literally, we may have to imagine an angel
nine hundred feet tall. I don't believe that is necessary.

More likely, the meaning of the angel's standing on
land and sea is that all of God's creation will be
embraced by his action! Everything in the world will
be affected by the Word of God. The angel's stance
emphasizes the all-inclusiveness of judgment.

The way this angel is described has made some
interpreters identify him as Christ. For one thing, he is
robed with a cloud. For another, he descends from
heaven. He holds the rainbow of promise, his fiery
legs speak of judgment and his face shines with the
glory of God.

But this does not mean the angel is Christ. Angels
proceed from heaven too, hence the cloud. They are
agents of the judgment of God and messengers of His
promises. Although the angel's face shone with the
glory of God, so did the face of Moses when he
returned from the top of Mount Sinai. Jesus is not an
angel, but the unique Son of God.

The angel brings a scroll in his hand. This one is
smaller than the scroll described in Revelation 5:1,

and it contains less writing. While the first scroll was sealed, this one lies unsealed and open. The proclamation of the Word of God has already begun, and therefore this scroll points to continued action. The scroll contains the prophetic word which John is supposed to announce (see v. 11).

The angel shouts with a loud voice like the roar of a lion. The emphasis here is on the volume. The voice is clearly heard—and feared—around the world.

Why do the "seven thunders" speak? That is another obscure detail, subject to conflicting interpretations. But the number seven means completeness, and thunder is loud! So presumably whatever was said was a definitive and forceful statement of God's purpose.

Whatever was declared is not disclosed. John has been given permission to share everything he has heard up till now—but now he is ordered to keep this knowledge hidden. Why? We don't know why. Speculation is useless; some things are simply not explained.

> Then the angel I had seen standing on the sea and on the land raised his right hand to heaven. And he swore by him who lives for ever and ever, who created the heavens and all that is in them, the earth and all that is in it, and the sea and all that is in it, and said, "There will be no more delay! But in the days when the seventh angel is about to sound his trumpet, the mystery of God will be accomplished, just as he announced to his servants the prophets" (10:5-7).

The angel raises his hand to heaven as if to take an oath. Oath taking seems like an unnecessary action for an angel, but the gesture emphasizes the importance of what is to follow.

At this juncture of world history the angel's message underscores once again the sovereignty of God. The Church is reminded that the Lord God, our Creator, is *at this moment* in control of the heavens and earth. And since God lives for ever and ever, He will continue in control.

And now we hear the answer to the first question: How long will the great tribulation last? Answer: "There will be no more delay." The message to the Church is: Take heart, all will soon be over! The finale is upon us! When the seventh trumpet sounds, the seven bowls will be poured out, and then will come the swan song.

As history draws to a conclusion, the mystery of God will be accomplished. "Mystery" in the New Testament does not imply a secret which remains hidden. It may have been a mystery for centuries, but it is now an open secret: "This mystery, which for ages past was kept hidden in God....His intent was that now through the church, the manifold wisdom of God should be made known" (Eph. 3:9,10). The mystery is the eternal purpose of God, which the New Testament discloses. That purpose is to be consummated at the end of world history!

> *Then the voice that I had heard from heaven spoke to me once more: "Go, take the scroll that lies open in the hand of the angel who is standing on the sea and on the land" (10:8).*

Who is speaking? The angel? God? Christ? We are told only that it is a "voice...from heaven,' and this fact conveys authority.

This same angel who stands on land and sea with the scroll in hand now gives the scroll to John and issues further instructions for the proclamation of the prophetic word.

> So I went to the angel and asked him to give me the little scroll. He said to me, "Take it and eat it. It will turn your stomach sour, but in your mouth it will be as sweet as honey." I took the little scroll from the angel's hand and ate it. It tasted as sweet as honey in my mouth, but when I had eaten it, my stomach turned sour. Then I was told, "You must prophesy again about many peoples, nations, languages and kings" (10: 9-11).

Like Ezekiel in the Old Testament, John was instructed to "eat the scroll." "Eating the Word" is a metaphor for receiving the Word in our hearts; prophets do not literally chew on paper.

Both Ezekiel and John testify that the Word tastes good. It is very sweet: the Word of God is full of promises. The good news of God is the Word of grace and mercy, of peace and love, of joy and hope. "Comfort, comfort my people, says your God" (Isa. 40:1).

Even as the gospel is sweet, however, the judgment is bitter. Judgment is the reverse side of grace. A prophet cannot avoid the preaching of judgment, even though he may not want to. That is why the scroll turns sour in the stomach.

John will proclaim the prophetic Word to the earth's inhabitants. This Word will be either *against* people or *about* people or *to* people. (The preposition in the original can be translated any of these ways.)

The same prophecy which is against or to the world is a Word of hope for the Church. Christians need never live in fear. We trust in the Lamb of God who has taken away our sin. Even now, He is standing near the throne. The Kingdom which He announced while here on earth will surely triumph! His coming is near! The Lord on the throne is in control.

The Two Witnesses

The last trumpet is delayed a little longer. We hear another message for the Church.

> *I was given a reed like a measuring rod and was told, "Go and measure the temple of God and the altar, and count the worshipers there. But exclude the outer court; do not measure it, because it has been given to the Gentiles. They will trample on the holy city for 42 months. And I will give power to my two witnesses, and they will prophesy for 1,260 days, clothed in sackcloth" (11:1-3).*

When John wrote these words, the Temple in Jerusalem was no longer standing. It had been destroyed by the Romans.

Why does John introduce the Temple here? Is this a gesture of good will toward the Jews? Will the Temple be restored in Jerusalem? What has this restoration to do with the Church? And why is he instructed to *measure* the Temple? The Bible already contains exact specifications in the Old Testament!

By now we have entered sufficiently into the spirit of the book of Revelation that we realize (with most commentators) that the Temple need not necessarily describe the actual Jewish temple in Jerusalem. "Temple" may be a symbol for "Church," a kind of code used to mislead the Romans. "Measuring the temple" can be likened to the sealing of the 144,000. This sealing or measuring is a means of protection for the Church during the tribulation. And the members are counted. This means God will give sanctuary to the faithful, even to individual Christians who are known personally, just as the hairs of our head are numbered.

The outer court is not guarded, however. It belongs to the "Gentiles." If the Temple represents the Church, perhaps the Gentiles symbolize Christians in name only, who are shaped more by the culture than by the Lord. They, like the rest of the world, will fall under the wrath of God, but the true Church will be preserved!

The outsiders, the world rulers, will trample down the city for a period of forty-two months—1260 days, or three and a half years. Are these literal days, months and years? John sounds very specific when he gives these figures, borrowing from the book of Daniel. Again, we are not required to make a precise interpretation of these numbers. We haven't done so earlier in Revelation!

These numbers represent an amount of time, a measured amount of time during which the world will persecute the Church. It is obvious that the Church has frequently suffered trials over the course of her history. The Gentiles have often "trampled on the holy city." But this is a special ordeal allotted by the sovereign Lord, who will protect the Church but not necessarily spare it from suffering.

And now two witnesses step forward. They prophesy and proclaim the Word. They are dressed in sack-cloth to underscore the seriousness of the proclamation during this tribulation. But who are these witnesses? And why are there two of them?

> *These are the two olive trees and the two lampstands that stand before the Lord of the earth. If anyone tries to harm them, fire comes from their mouths and devours their enemies. This is how anyone who wants to harm them must die. These men have power to shut up the sky so that it will not rain during the time they are prophesying; and they have power to turn the waters into blood and to strike the earth with every kind of plague as often as they want (11:4-6).*

The two witnesses are modeled after Moses and Elijah. Moses representing the law, Elijah the prophets. Like Moses, they are able to turn water into blood and strike the earth with plagues. Like Elijah, these witnesses are able to control the weather through prayer. These obvious comparisons point to the witnesses appearing in the power of Moses and Elijah. I do not believe, however, as a few commentators hold, that Moses and Elijah will actually be physically resurrected. These witnesses are not named.

Why are they called olive trees? The figure of speech is taken from the prophet Zechariah, who explains that the leaders of his time are as fruitful olive trees.

Lampstands? We have encountered lampstands in Revelation 1:20. They signify the churches.

These pictures, therefore, provide us with mixed metaphors. Are these two individual prophets who preach in the last days, or are these two churches? Does the number two refer to Christian Jews and Gentile Christians? Why is there not just one prophet? Why not seven—as in the seven churches?

We are at a loss in the maze of this symbolic language. How can we make sense of the symbolism?

When we ask the important question, "what is the point?" we will come closer to the truth. Here are two witnesses for the Lord, whether individuals or churches, who epitomize the Church. They speak for the Lord. What they are doing is more important than who they are! Their presence tells us that *it is more important to witness for the Lord than to peer into mysteries we cannot decipher.*

The Church must witness to the world. That is true for all Christians from the first century until now! What is the purpose of the Church? To maintain a steady witness until the end of time.

Out of mouth of the two prophets emanates fire. This represents the Word of God, not actual flames. Jesus came to bring fire on earth. The gospel proclaimed by the Church is the Word of power, of fire. Satan will be defeated by the vigor of the Word. The gates of Hades will not prevail against the Church! (Matt.16:18)

Now when they have finished their testimony, the beast that comes up from the Abyss will attack them, and overpower and kill them (11:7).

The authority of the two witnesses is broken. The testimony of the Church draws to an end. The hour of prophecy is concluded when "the beast" arises from the Abyss. There will be more details about the beast later. At this point, it is sufficient for us to note that "the beast" is not identified as animal, human, angel or demon. Nor is he "a" beast, that is any old beast, but "the" specific beast who emerges out of the bottomless pit, that is, from among the demons. The beast has received power to destroy the witnesses.

> *Their bodies will lie in the street of the great city, which is figuratively called Sodom and Egypt, where also their Lord was crucified. For three and a half days men from every people, tribe, language and nation will gaze on their bodies and refuse them burial. The inhabitants of the earth will gloat over them and will celebrate by sending each other gifts, because these two prophets had tormented those who live on the earth (11:8-10).*

It is a great insult to leave bodies lying in the street in the near East. People are buried the same day they die. Because the climate is hot, there is no embalming and no waiting period. But in this scenario, the bodies are left to rot in the open.

The city where this occurs is figuratively called Sodom for its sin and Egypt for its idolatry. (It is not unusual for Hebrew prophets to speak in this manner.) John tells us unequivocally that this is the city where "their Lord was crucified"—that is, Jerusalem. But this does not necessarily mean the actual city of Jerusalem. John was specific about mentioning the Temple; now he is specific about Jerusalem. But if the Temple delineates the Church, the city could symbolize something larger—even the whole world.

If we accept this allegorical interpretation, we get a vivid picture of a depraved society. Sodom signifies all that is foul and polluted in the world. Egypt illustrates idolatry and oppression, like Rome. And Jerusalem connotes the world which crucified Christ. Looked at in this way, the passage would mean that Christians become the butt of public scorn *in every city*. The persecution of the Church explodes worldwide!

The bodies of the witnesses remain stinking in the streets for three and a half days—a measured amount of time. How can people from around the world view these bodies in so short a time span? Imaginative interpreters in the twentieth century have a ready answer: television.

The world gloats over the misfortune of Christians. The people of the world rejoice over the defeat of the Church. Everyone joins in the celebration with an exchange of gifts. It's Christmas in July—or whatever. The book of Revelation is not optimistic about human nature!

But why do the witnesses cause "torment" to the inhabitants of earth? What the Church proclaims is the pure and powerful gospel of Jesus Christ. Does the Word of God cause torment to the world because it exposes and condemns the immoralities, the liberties and the idolatries of people? The fire of the gospel kindles the judgment of God on the evils of society. And society reacts with scorn and persecution.

But God is not finished yet:

> But after the three and a half days a breath of life from God entered them, and they stood on their feet, and terror struck those who saw them. Then they heard a loud voice from heaven saying to them, "Come up here." And they went up to heaven in a cloud, while their enemies looked on (11:11,12).

The Church is resurrected! At certain times in history, the Church has been knocked down and out, only to rise again. Christians have been imprisoned and slain, churches closed, Bibles burned, then suddenly a spiritual renewal erupts. Like the dry bones of Ezekiel's prophecy (see Ezek. 37), what seemed dead has come to life. And now a great miracle touches the entire world. The reaction to the resurrection is a mixture of terror and awe.

In the meantime, the Church is invited to enter heaven. As the world looks on the witnesses are taken up. A very public rapture. Is this "the taking up of the Church," or is John saying in a picturesque way that those who believe in the Lord will be raised to live eternally with Him? Commentators disagree. Whatever the meaning, however, surely this is a word of hope and comfort for the Church!

> *At that same moment there was a violent earthquake, and a tenth of the city fell. Seven thousand people were killed in the earthquake; the rest in terror did homage to the God of heaven. The second woe has now passed. But the third is soon to come (11:13,14, NEB).*

There are signs in nature. This is God in action! A giant earthquake strikes panic in people's hearts. Seven thousand people are killed. Seven is the perfect number; 1000 a number of completion: 7 x 1000 = 7000. Is a whole city devastated? A country? What is the literal or figurative interpretation of 7000? We can only speculate. But the devastation is clearly massive.

Now, for the first time in the book of Revelation,

something new and exciting happens. The world responds to God! It is a response motivated by fear, to be sure, but it is a response. People actually give glory to God now that the foundations are shaking under their feet. They acknowledge God as God. Do they become Christians? We can't be sure, but their stubborn resistance is broken.

The Seventh Trumpet

The seventh angel sounded his trumpet, and there were loud voices in heaven, which said:

"The kingdom of the world has become the kingdom of our Lord and of his Christ,
*   and he will reign forever and ever" (11:15,16).*

Finally! This is the time of victory! The Kingdom of Jesus Christ arrives!

Following the seventh seal there was silence in heaven. In contrast, following the seventh trumpet we hear loud voices, triumphant voices, voices praising the Lord and giving thanks for His sovereign rule.

The kingdom of the world is temporal. The kingdom of God is eternal. His reign is without end. This is the fulfillment of His promise. This is our hope. And this is the present security for those who trust in Jesus Christ.

And the twenty-four elders, who were seated on their thrones before God, fell on their faces and worshiped God, saying:

"We give thanks to you, Lord God Almighty,
     the One who is and who was,
because you have taken your great power
     and have begun to reign.
The nations were angry;
     and your wrath has come.
The time has come for judging the dead,
     and for rewarding your servants the prophets
and your saints and those who rever-
               ence your name,
     both small and great—
and for destroying those who destroy the earth"
(11:16-18).

The elders don't get to sit very much! They are always falling down to worship the living God. But there's a new note to their worship now. They praise "One who is and who was"—not the "One who is to come." Earlier in Revelation, the Eternal was announced as coming, but now He has appeared in judgment, and the final scenario is in progress. The world trembles under the hand of the Almighty, and the reign of God is visible over the horizon. The light of a new day is dawning.

But there is yet a little more that must take place. More wrath will be poured out with the seven bowls. God will reveal His majesty. Hostile powers are to be judged and subdued, and then the kingdom of God will appear.

Christians will be rewarded. The servants of the Lord, the saints of the most High and all those who honor the Lamb will be recompensed. The blessings of God are for the Church universal; they are not confined to a chosen few.

*Then God's temple in heaven was opened, and with-
in his temple was seen the ark of his covenant. And
there came flashes of lightning, rumblings, peals of
thunder, an earthquake and a great hailstorm
(11:19).*

At this point we are given a glimpse of the temple
in heaven, which represents God's presence, and the
chest of the covenant, which stands for His promises.

God is the covenant-keeping God. He made a
covenant with Abraham which He has always kept.
He made a new covenant through Jesus Christ which
He can be trusted to preserve. This is the Word of
comfort for the Church as more signs in creation
strike the earth: lightning, thunders, rumblings, earthquakes and storms. And all the while the kingdom of
God, announced by Jesus and reaffirmed by His apostles, stands in the wings, ready to come on stage.

Questions for Discussion and Meditation

1. How can we actually *eat* the word of God (the
   scroll)?

2. What is the importance of the time element (42
   months, etc.) in relation to the tribulation?

3. Why is there rejoicing over the death of the witnesses?

4. How can you maintain the attitude of thanksgiving
   and worship in times of trial?

CHAPTER EIGHT

The Woman and the Dragon

Revelation 12

Something new happens in the book of Revelation at
this point. Consequently, some commentators have
divided the book into two parts: chapters 1 through 11
and 12 through 21. One thing is clear: Chapter 12 pictures a scene which allows us a look behind the curtain! It provides us with insight concerning what has
already transpired on earth and also gives us a peek
into the meaning of future events! These dramatic
scenes explain why the Church is persecuted, why
Christians suffer, and what God is accomplishing in
His eternal purpose.

Why is there continual hostility against believers?
Why are Christians the object of so much oppression?
The curtain is pulled away, and we are introduced to
the actors who play major roles in the drama.

The Woman

*A great and wondrous sign appeared in heaven: a
woman clothed with the sun, with the moon under*

her feet and a crown of twelve stars on her head. She
was pregnant and cried out in pain as she was about
to give birth (12:1,2).

Who is this woman? Israel, who gives birth to the
Christ child? Or Mary, the mother of Jesus? Both
views have been advanced.

As we read on, several facts become clear. The child
the woman bears is the Savior of the world. Therefore,
the woman represents the community of believers
which produced this child—that is, Israel. But the
woman is also persecuted, just as the Church experiences persecution. And like the church, she is nourished and protected by the Lord in times of trouble. I
think it most likely that the woman symbolizes believers who trust in the Lamb. She represents both the
faithful of the Old Testament, and the Christians who
live under the new covenant.

The woman is clothed with the sun, which in the
Bible typifies righteousness. (For example, Malachi
4:2 speaks of "the sun of righteousness," a reference to
the coming Messiah.) The woman therefore signifies
those who have put on the righteousness of the Lord.
(The saved community does not trust in its own righteousness.)

The moon is under her feet; she has been given
dominion. The twelve stars on her head could represent the twelve tribes of Israel, since, after all, the
Messiah came from Israel.

The Dragon

Then another sign appeared in heaven: an enormous
red dragon with seven heads and ten horns and

seven crowns on his heads. His tail swept a third of
the stars out of the sky and flung them to the earth.
The dragon stood in front of the woman who was
about to give birth, so that he might devour her child
the moment it was born (12:3,4).

The dragon is the devil (see v. 9). Why is Satan pictured as a dragon? Because dragons were greatly feared in ancient times. They were considered powerful, frightening and, above all, mysterious. Ordinary people had no means of confronting dragons—much less conquering them. Like the devil, a dragon is cryptic, dangerous and the enemy of all that is good.

This dragon is enormous, the more to be feared. He is red, the color of blood. He makes war and is bent on destruction!

He has seven heads, seven crowns. Seven makes a complete number. Heads indicate vitality and power. Crowns represent authority and dominion, as do horns, which typify nations and tribes. The dragon has ten horns. These probably do not mean ten actual nations. Instead, they signify that *the whole world* serves the dragon! Only Christians are loyal to the Lamb! The nations of the world bring their energy and allegiance to Satan. He has absolute authority on earth.

Dragons have tails, of course. The tail of this mighty dragon sweeps cartoon-like over the sky, and a third of the stars fall from the heavens. This shows he has the ability to affect the elements.

But what is the dragon seeking to accomplish? He wants to destroy the child who is about to be born! He stands in front of the woman and waits for the birth of the baby. Why does he not destroy the woman before she brings forth her son? Because the faithful enjoy the Lord's protection! God is in control, not the dragon. God keeps His own from the attack of the enemy.

The Child

And the child? The dragon makes an attempt to slay the baby, but He is also protected. To me and to many commentators, this seems to be a reference to events surrounding the birth of Jesus. He was spirited away by His parents to Egypt before the infants in and around Bethlehem were annihilated by King Herod.

John emphasizes that the purpose of God overrides the vicious assaults of the dragon:

> *She gave birth to a son, a male child, who will rule all the nations with an iron scepter. And her child was snatched up to God and to his throne. The woman fled into the desert to a place prepared for her by God, where she might be taken care of for 1,260 days (12:5,6).*

The male child born to the woman is clearly Jesus. And it is distinctly stated that He will eventually rule the world—he will rule with an "iron scepter." This destiny was announced at Jesus' birth (see Luke 1:32,33) and foretold in the Old Testament (see Psalm 2, which predicts the strength and certainty of the Messiah's reign). Jesus Himself spoke of His destiny in His message to the church at Thyatira (see Rev. 2:27).

Since His destiny is to reign as King, nothing is said of Jesus' earthly ministry. Even in His infancy, He is pictured as He will be: the exalted Lord. The emphasis is on His triumphant ascension to the throne, the climax of all He achieved on earth. The risen Lord is *now* on the throne. This is the Lord in whom we believe and whom we trust.

And so we see that even from the beginning, Satan's plan has been foiled. The sovereign God was always in command.

And now the woman—the believing community—flees into the desert. The purpose is to escape from the domain of the dragon, to get out from under the pressure of the hostile world. The Church retreats to safety and solidarity. The desert could stand for a state of spiritual safety and not necessarily an actual terrain. As Jesus said, we are to be *in* the world, but not *of* the world.

As the Lord fed Israel in the wilderness after the Exodus, so He will nourish His Church during the time of trouble. Those Christians who are not removed from the world will be protected in the world.

The number given for the duration of the tribulation is 1260 days. There's that number again: forty-two months, or three and a half years, or 1260 days. By now we have made it clear that numbers in the book of Revelation are not intended to be literal, but we can be sure that this is a *measured* period. At all times, but especially during times of tribulation we are able to put our complete trust in our Lord and Savior. Our fate and our future are always in His hands!

War in Heaven

Then war broke out in heaven. Michael and his angels waged war upon the dragon. The dragon and his angels fought, but they had not the strength to win, and no foothold was left them in heaven. So the great dragon was thrown down, that serpent of old that led the whole world astray, whose name is Satan, or the Devil—thrown down to the earth, and his angels with him (12:7-9, NEB).

The dragon stands exposed. His identity is unveiled. The dragon is the serpent who tempted Adam and Eve in the garden of Eden. He is Satan, who tested Jesus in the wilderness, and whom Jesus called a liar and a murderer (see John 8:44). Satan is the hidden power behind the powers on earth. He controls the culture; he establishes false goals and values and leads the whole world astray.

The Old Testament teaches that Satan is a fallen angel. He was created good but aspired to have the power and sovereignty of God. Therefore he was cast out of heaven: "How you are fallen from heaven, O Lucifer, son of the morning!" (Isa. 14:12, NKJV). But Satan did not give up after his expulsion. He apparently still had access to heaven, where he brutally accused the righteous before the throne of God (see for example Job 1:6-11).

But now it is over—the final expulsion of Satan! There will be no more access to the throne, no more slander of the saints. The dragon loses the battle against the angel Michael—the guardian angel of Israel (see Dan. 12:1)—and has to vacate heaven.

Jesus foretold the event: "I saw Satan fall like lightning from heaven" (Luke 10:18).

Satan's descent from heaven has great significance for Christians! The devil is no longer able to accuse the servants of the Lord before God. We can breathe freely. Satan's defeat leaves only the earth as his sphere of operation. But he will make the most of it. These are his last days!

> *Then I heard a loud voice in heaven say:*
>
> *Now have come the salvation and the power and the*
>   *kingdom of our God,*
>   *and the authority of his Christ.*
> *For the accuser of our brothers,*
>   *who accuses them before our God day and night,*
>   *has been hurled down.*
> *They overcame him*
>   *by the blood of the Lamb*
>   *and by the word of their testimony;*
> *they did not love their lives so much*
>   *as to shrink from death.*
> *Therefore rejoice, you heavens*
>   *and you who dwell in them!*
> *But woe to the earth and the sea,*
>   *because the devil has gone down to you!*
> *He is filled with fury,*
>   *because he knows that his time is short*
>   *(12:10-12).*

With the expulsion of Satan from heaven, salvation for God's people is assured. The time has come. The Kingdom is near. The earth will bear the ravages of evil only for a little while longer. This is the message for the followers of the Lamb: "Lift up your heads, because your redemption is drawing near" (Luke 21:28). Your hope is in God!

With this message of hope, we see *how* Christians gain the victory, both now and in the future:

"By the blood of the Lamb." We trust in the sacrifice of Jesus Christ for the forgiveness of sins and the gift of eternal life. We are accepted through the death of Jesus on the cross. We are washed clean "by the blood of the Lamb," and we live by the grace of God, reconciled to God by the cross.

"By the word of their testimony." We are to believe on the Lord Jesus Christ, to hold on to our salvation, to retain the truth, and to keep the faith. We are to persevere in the word and to be faithful, no matter how fierce the opposition.

"They did not shrink from death." Faithfulness to the Lord extends, if need be, unto death! Death cannot end our life, for we have been promised eternal life through Jesus Christ. Christians are willing to sacrifice their lives, trusting the risen Lord and believing in the resurrection of the dead.

Satan is cast out—and therefore joy in heaven, fury on earth.

Conflict on Earth

> *When the dragon saw that he had been hurled to the earth, he pursued the woman who had given birth to the male child.The woman was given the two wings of a great eagle, so that she might fly to the place prepared for her in the desert, where she would be taken care of for a time, times and half a time, out of the serpent's reach (12:13,14).*

Satan does not give up, even though his days are numbered! He is the enemy of God. Therefore, the object of his hostility is the Christian community, which openly confesses allegiance to the Lord.

The faithful are nourished by the Lord in the desert. Perhaps the desert symbolizes those lonely places where we must stand up to the tides of public opinion and live in opposition to the godless, materialistic world. But we are not alone "in the desert." The Lord has promised to protect us—to be with us always, even to the end of the age (see Matt. 28:20). He has never promised we will be spared from persecution.

The eagle wings given to the woman are another form of the Lord's protection. The picture of the eagle need not refer to an actual airlift, as some writers claim, unless you want to make the Exodus under Moses an airlift, too! "You yourselves have seen what I did to Egypt, and how I carried you on eagles' wings and brought you to myself" (Exod. 19:4). God delivered Israel out of Egypt and shepherded them through the wilderness. In like manner, He will save the Church during times of trouble. This is His word of comfort to Christians. It is good until the very end!

The period of distress during which the woman is protected in the desert endures for "a time, times and half a time." Perhaps this is another way of expressing three and a half years: time (1) plus times (2) plus half a time (1/2) equals three and a half, the block of time spoken of as the period of tribulation upon earth (see Rev. 12:5,6). But the faithful will be secure during that time. They will abide "under God's wings," no matter what happens.

This is wonderful assurance for all who trust the Lord!

Then from his mouth the serpent spewed water like a river, to overtake the woman and sweep her away with the torrent. But the earth helped the woman by

> *opening its mouth and swallowing the river that the*
> *dragon had spewed out of his mouth. Then the drag-*
> *on was enraged at the woman and went off to make*
> *war against the rest of her offspring—those who*
> *obey God's commandments and hold to the testimo-*
> *ny of Jesus (12:15-17).*

Now the dragon is determined to destroy the woman, the Christian community. From his mouth comes "water like a river." What is this "water," which is intended to drown the Church?

Some commentators believe that water represents people, the people of the world. They point out, in addition, that in Scripture water is sometimes a symbol of overwhelming evil (Isa. 43:2). The rushing river could thus represent an almost overwhelming tide of secularism and worldliness. But the earth, the creation of God, swallows the water and saves the believers. This is clearly a reference to the rescue of Israel when the Red Sea opened to let Israel escape from the Egyptians.

Others interpret the waters as the sweeping power of lies and false teaching. The lies of the enemy attempt to infiltrate the believing community, so that Christians wonder what they are supposed to believe. But such false teachings are swallowed by the truth of the Word. The Church will not turn to heresy. The Word of God triumphs over the deceptions of the devil.

The Lord helps us, but Satan does not stop!

He now wages war against the offspring of the woman—Christians who follow the Lamb until the end of time. As long as we are in the flesh, we will continue to be the focus of Satan's hostility.

In face of all these temptations, we are to keep the commandments of God. We are to hold to the testimony Jesus gave—the Word of the Lord to the Church! The book of Revelation is written to encourage all believers to remain faithful. We can put our trust in the purpose of the sovereign Lord. His Kingdom will triumph!

And the dragon stood on the shore of the sea (13:1).

The dragon now takes his position in the world, ready to unleash his worst. What is yet to come is even more frightening than what has already happened.

Questions for Discussion and Meditation

1. What insight do you gain from this chapter about:

   (a) the devil?

   (b) the Church?

   (c) the time element?

   (d) the purpose of God?

2. How can Christians live by hope?

3. What does the protection of God mean to the Church today? For you personally?

CHAPTER NINE

The Two Beasts and the Church

Revelation 13 and 14

Picture a frightening, horrifying creature which combines the savagery and ferocity of the animal world with the barbarity of the demonic, and you have "the beast" of Revelation.

The Beast from the Sea

> And I saw a beast coming out of the sea. He had ten horns and seven heads, with ten crowns on his horns, and on each head a blasphemous name. The beast I saw resembled a leopard, but had feet like those of a bear and a mouth like that of a lion. The dragon gave the beast his power and his throne and great authority (13:1,2).

John sees emerging from the sea what he calls a beast, which for him and his first-century readers no doubt represents the Roman empire. (The early

Christians dared not make such an identification openly.)

From our perspective, we expect the beast to represent more than Rome. Through the centuries, many conquerors have overpowered other nations. This last beast symbolizes a heathen empire which will rule supreme over the world at the very end of human history.

As the beast emerges from the water, we see first the horns breaking water. The horns typify world leaders, possibly a kind of "United Nations" brought together under one authority. They number ten, a complete number. Following the horns, seven heads swim into view. Seven is also a complete number; the seven heads indicate total dominion. Furthermore, each horn is crowned. The crowns express power and authority, perhaps in imitation of the Lamb, who alone is crowned King of kings.

This world power openly opposes the Lord. On each head is written a blasphemous name. No one can mistake the intent of the beast.

Now the entire beast emerges, and the first impression is of a leopard, swift and ferocious. But the feet resemble those of a bear, who can strike with its powerful paws and wound anyone in its path. And when the beast opens his mouth, he exposes the deadly teeth of a lion!

In the book of Daniel, the author pictures world empires, describing one kingdom as being like a leopard, another like a lion, a third like a bear. In the book of Revelation, the three deadly creatures have been combined into one stupendous, dreadful power!

The dragon (Satan) gives to the beast, which rules the world, its throne and authority. This is how evil empires receive their power—from the devil! The world in which Christians live and move is demonic, an extension of Satan's domain. Evil opposes the good; therefore the prime focus of the beast's anger is the people of God. Christians can expect to experience trouble in the world. In fact, Jesus warned us about persecution if we follow Him (see John 16:33).

> *One of the heads of the beast seemed to have had a fatal wound, but the fatal wound had been healed. The whole world was astonished and followed the beast. Men worshiped the dragon because he had given authority to the beast, and they also worshiped the beast and asked, "Who is like the beast? Who can make war against him?" (13:3,4).*

There are those who identify this beast as the Antichrist, spoken of elsewhere in Scripture as a "man of lawlessness" who will be able to unite the whole world under his program (see Daniel 11:36-45; 2 Thess. 2:8-12; 1 John 2:18-29; 2 John 7-11). His evil policy is in direct opposition to the Lord; it is anti-Christ in every sense. And what is worse, the world believes in and follows "the beast."

Both the beast and the devil are worshiped by the world. Human beings incline toward the worship of something. If they refuse to praise the true God, they will inevitably turn to the false. The book of Revelation unmasks false worship. Christians are reminded that the one whom the world follows is none other than Satan. The message is strong and clear: Continue serving the Lord! Only the Lamb on the throne is worthy of our adoration!

The world leader is admired because of his ability

to heal. He has even overcome a seemingly fatal wound. There is no indication that it actually *was* a fatal wound, however. The beast did not sacrifice himself like the Lamb of God; neither did he rise from the dead. But the world is fooled by this shoddy imitation of the crucified and risen Lord and follows the false world leader blindly.

With the authority of Satan and the persuasion of fake miracles, the power of the world leader becomes absolute. No one dares oppose his despotic rule on earth. Only Christians are able to see through the glossy veneer to the evil intent.

> *The beast was given a mouth to utter proud words and blasphemies and to exercise his authority for forty-two months. He opened his mouth to blaspheme God, and to slander his name and his dwelling place and those who live in heaven. He was given power to make war against the saints and to conquer them. And he was given authority over every tribe, people, language and nation. All inhabitants of the earth will worship the beast—all whose names have not been written in the book of life belonging to the Lamb that was slain from the creation of the world. He who has an ear, let him hear (13:5-9).*

The beast demonstrates other characteristics of the Antichrist. He is proud and blasphemous. He slanders God and the people of God. He speaks against the saints in heaven and the saints on earth. Nothing constructive nor good proceeds from his mouth. He does not create; he can only destroy.

Since the object of the beast's wrath is the believing community, the whole world joins in victimizing

believers! Not one nation nor tribe withholds its allegiance from the beast. All those whose names are not
recorded in the Lamb's book of life rally against the
people of God.

Once again we are reminded that believers will not
escape persecution from the world nor attacks from
the devil. Christians must be willing to endure the trials that will come upon them, but we can take comfort
in the promise that the tribulation will last only a limited period of time. The time has been set—the period
established by the Lord. And through every moment
of the test, we are promised we will be safe in the
hands of our merciful, sovereign Lord.

Given the fact of suffering, this is the choice: We can
offer allegiance to the beast who inflicts suffering or to
the Lamb who accepts suffering. We can trust either in
proud world rulers or in the Lamb who was slain
from the foundation of the world. There is no in-
between. We are constantly confronted with eternal
choices!

That is why the Word to the seven churches is
repeated at this crucial point in history: "He who has
an ear, let him hear." God is speaking to His people
even in the worst of times. His word is full of comfort
indeed, when we hear what He wants to say to us.

> *If anyone is to go into captivity,*
> *into captivity he will go.*
> *If anyone is to be killed with the sword,*
> *with the sword he will be killed.*

> *This calls for patient endurance and faithfulness on*
> *the part of the saints (13:10).*

When we follow the Lord, prison may become our lot. Perhaps we will suffer a martyr's death. No matter what will happen, we need a faith that will see us through. If at present you are not put to the test, it is well to prepare, to strengthen your faith, to practice patience and perseverance. Read the holy Word of God, worship, pray and fellowship with the people of God.

As the end of history approaches, the power of the beast becomes even more absolute. No individual Christian nor fellowship of believers is able to subdue the dragon or the beast. Only Christ will gain the victory. In Him we put our trust. He is our only hope. We await the dawning of a new day.

The Beast from the Earth

Then I saw another beast, coming out of the earth. He had two horns like a lamb, but he spoke like a dragon. He exercised all the authority of the first beast on his behalf, and made the earth and its inhabitants worship the first beast, whose fatal wound had been healed (13:11,12).

What, *another* beast? Isn't the first one enough? We already have a dragon (Satan) who gives power to a beast (the Antichrist) that surfaces from the sea. Now comes the second beast, and it emerges from the earth. The earth is viewed here not as God's creation, but as the realm of the godless society.

Some identify this second beast as "the false prophet." This is because he operates more in the religious realm than in the political. But all he says and does underlines the authority of the first beast, the supreme commander. He is the world ruler's minister of propaganda (director of public relations?) or perhaps secretary of state, and he will end up by causing the world to worship the beast.

We have here an unholy trinity: the dragon, the first beast and the second beast; Satan, the Antichrist and the false prophet.

This beast from the earth sports two lamblike horns, imitating the Lamb of God, but his words betray him. He sounds like the devil; his words are compared to the dragon! He is a prophet not from above, but from below. He is demonic—a wolf in sheep's clothing.

> *And he performed great and miraculous signs, even causing fire to come down from heaven to earth in full view of men. Because of the signs he was given power to do on behalf of the first beast, he deceived the inhabitants of the earth. He ordered them to set up an image in honor of the beast who was wounded by the sword and yet lived. He was given power to give breath to the image of the first beast, so that it could speak and cause all who refused to worship the image to be killed (13:13-15).*

The power to do miracles is given to the false prophet not by God, but by the devil, who is a master of deception: "Satan himself masquerades as an angel of light" (2 Cor. 11:14). The whole world is taken in by these fake miracles, as they were initially taken in by the beast's imitation of resurrection. When Jesus was in the world, very few believed in His true signs. Now the multitude is willing to accept the false!

After this, the lying prophet establishes the worship of the Antichrist—the false standards and worldly goals paraded by our culture. The idols of money, sex, power and pleasure are universally espoused. Temporal, not eternal values predominate. Self-indulgence instead of self-sacrifice is the order of the day.

The deceiver of the world has deceived all those whose names are not written in the book of life! They fail to accept the truth because they prefer to stick with the lie.

People who are without Christ worship whatever they are told! Whatever "gods" the devil anoints are followed foolishly, because "the god of this age has blinded the minds of unbelievers" (2 Cor. 4:4). Let Christians beware of the dangers and remain alert in the Lord!

And now the world is accorded a neat trick. The statue of the Antichrist begins to talk! Anyone who refuses to acknowledge this miracle and will not worship the supreme idol will die. Christians who stubbornly resist bowing down to the gods of the world are in grave danger.

In the Roman world, making statues talk was a well-known sorcerer's device. Whether they used ventriloquism or other tricks, who knows? Our reason tells us that statues were unable to speak of themselves. And this will continue to be true, even though we possess electronic devices which can make robots do amazing things.

The point is, neutrality is impossible! Christians will be put to the supreme test in an antichristian world. If your name is written in the book of life, take heart. You can do nothing better than be bold in your commitment, hold on to your faith in the living Lord and trust the Lamb on the throne!

He also forced everyone, small and great, rich and poor, free and slave, to receive a mark on his right hand or on his forehead, so that no one could buy or sell unless he had the mark, which is the name of the beast or the number of his name. This calls for wisdom. If anyone has insight, let him calculate the number of the beast, for it is man's number. His number is 666 (13:16-18).

The beast's right-hand man enforces universal obedience. All people on earth, no matter what their status, receive the mark of the beast. This identifying feature will be either on the forehead, (probably a symbol for the mind) or on the hand (which symbolizes action); it will enable everyone to buy and sell. Those who are not the people of God sell out to the beast and the dragon, body and soul. There is no neutral zone.

- Christians will not be marked, for they are sealed.
- It is better to obtain a seal than a mark.
- A mark is for identification. A seal means belonging.
- A mark provides power to buy and sell. A seal brings protection.
- A mark is a parody of a seal.

Once again, John is speaking symbolically. People probably won't actually be marked on their bodies, but they will have some form of identification which enables them to do business—perhaps some form of government bank card. Without such identification, there is almost no chance to survive, economically or in any other way!

The point is that the devil with his worldly agents, the beast out of the sea and the beast from the earth, take over and control the entire world! Everything becomes enemy territory. Christians are no longer welcome anywhere. And they feel the pressure.

Nevertheless, those who are sealed by Christ will not accept the mark of the beast. We may be tempted and fall, but in the long run, having received the Holy Spirit, we will not "sell our soul" for earthly gratification. It is not possible to accept both the Lord *and* the dragon and his deputies. We cannot serve God and material goals at the same time (Matt. 6:24).

But how will Christians recognize the mark of the beast? John says this calls for wisdom—discernment. Then he tells us that we can recognize the beast by his number—666.

Who then, is the Antichrist, the beast? And what is the meaning of this mysterious number?

There has been more speculation about the number 666 than probably any other image in Revelation. In the first century, John knew what 666 meant to the early Church. By the second century, the interpretation had already been lost! No one has been able to recapture the identity of the number. There have been guesses in every age, so that *hundreds* of famous world figures and leaders have been accorded the dubious distinction of being labeled as the Antichrist!

But the passage itself contains a clue: "It is man's number." Man's, not God's. If seven is a perfect number and represents God, six is just a little less than seven; it stands for humanity.

The Antichrist epitomizes the number 666. Three sixes, a trinity of sixes, means mankind to the nth degree—total humanity without God.

Six describes failure, missing the mark. Six illustrates the world, not heaven—the human, not the divine. Failure upon failure upon failure deepens the impression that humankind is doomed, apart from God. God and God alone will triumph.

That is the real "wisdom" to which this passage of Revelation points: Christians should aim for seven rather than six. Christians, saved by our Lord Jesus Christ, are to live not in their own strength, but in the power of the Holy Spirit.

And the Church

And now we come to a striking vision which is meant to give all Christians *assurance!*

> *Then I looked, and there before me was the Lamb, standing on Mount Zion, and with him 144,000 who had his name and his Father's name written on their foreheads. And I heard a sound from heaven like the roar of rushing waters and like a loud peal of thunder. The sound I heard was like that of harpists playing their harps. And they sang a new song before the throne and before the four living creatures and the elders. No one could learn the song except the 144,000 who had been redeemed from the earth (14:1-3).*

The Lamb is still on Mount Zion. He has not disappeared during the onslaught of the dragon and the two beasts. He is standing, which means that He is still active. The judgment of God has not been completed. Jesus is not yet seated.

Mount Zion is the original hill on which the city of Jerusalem was built, and the name "Zion" is used throughout the Bible to stand for the city of

Jerusalem. But there is no implication here that Jesus has returned to the earthly Jerusalem. Rather, Mount Zion symbolizes the heavenly Jerusalem, the city of the living God (Heb. 12:22).

As shown in Revelation 7, the 144,000 represent those who believe in Jesus Christ as Lord and Savior, from both the old and the new dispensation: 12 (tribes of Israel) x 12 (apostles) x 1000 (a complete, perfect number). What is significant about this vision is that the 144,000 are with the Lamb. The Body of Christ is visible in heaven. They have potentially made it through the tribulation. *No one has been lost!* Those who were sealed were kept by the Lord.

This is pure encouragement for Christians to refuse "the mark of the beast" and remain true to "their Father's name written on their foreheads." Those who reject the world's false goals and remain faithful to the Lamb are promised a place in the eternal kingdom of God.

The faithful sing a new song, the song of redemption, which is known only by the saints of the most High. It is so beautiful that John has difficulty describing it. He tries using picture language: rushing waters, peals of thunder, harpists playing harps. But then he admits that the images fall short of the reality! The magnificence of the song is beyond delineation.

> *These are those who did not defile themselves with women, for they kept themselves pure. They follow the Lamb wherever he goes. They were purchased from among men and offered as firstfruits to God and the Lamb. No lie was found in their mouths; they are blameless (14:4,5).*

These are the saints—the Church of the living God. This is not a privileged group which receives special awards for meritorious works. The 144,000 represent the entire Body of Christ.

What, then, is the meaning of their "virginity"? If they have not defiled themselves with women, are they celibate believers? Holier than others? Or, for that matter, are they all men?

The meaning of "purity" goes beyond the physical. The purity which characterizes believers is spiritual. To "not defile themselves with women" expresses holy worship in symbolic language and is not limited to men! Christians do not copy the world in bowing down to idols. John goes on to explain the purity of the 144,000: "They follow the Lamb wherever he goes." The fact that they do not lie means they do not accept the lie, the false, the Satanic, but stubbornly stick to the truth. They are obedient to the Lamb and do not succumb to earthly temptation.

To understand this, it is important to realize that sexual purity—which includes marital fidelity—is used to symbolize spiritual purity and faithfulness throughout the Bible. Israel is called "the Virgin daughter of Zion" (2 Kings 19:21), although she is married to the Lord: "Your Maker is your husband—the Lord Almighty is his name" (Isa. 54:5). In seeking other lovers, which implies following after false gods, the wife of Jehovah is said to have "played the harlot" (Hos. 2:5, NKJV).

Later in the book of Revelation (21:9), the Church is called the Bride of Christ. She is presented to Him blameless and pure because she has not accepted other lovers. This means she has not received the mark of the beast nor committed adultery with the world (17:2). The Church has taken John's admonition to heart: "Dear children, keep yourselves from idols" (1 John 5:21).

Spiritual purity is the goal of the Church! And so is truthfulness, the virtue which follows on the heels of purity. ("No lie was found in their mouths.")

The inspiration Christians receive from this heavenly vision is to be lived out in the world. We have been purchased by the Lamb and are invited to follow our Lord down the narrow way to eternal life. We are called to be saints. We are the bride of Christ.

Three Angels

> *I saw another angel flying in midair, and he had the eternal gospel to proclaim to those who live on the earth—to every nation, tribe, language and people. He said in a loud voice, "Fear God and give him glory, because the hour of his judgment has come. Worship him who made the heavens, the earth, the sea and the springs of water" (14:6,7).*

Here is the final appeal to the world: Worship the true God of the universe! The last judgment is about to fall. Salvation lies in giving glory to the sovereign Lord.

The voice of the angel is loud so that everyone will hear. The message is for the whole earth.

This is the only mention of the eternal gospel in the book of Revelation. The good news, which announces both the judgment and the grace of God, is eternal in that it is always true. The gospel is eternal because the mercy of the Lord extends to all generations. Even now, as the sun is about to go down, God's grace is available for the people of earth. It is not too late to seek the Lord.

> *A second angel followed and said, "Fallen! Fallen is Babylon the Great, which made all the nations drink the maddening wine of her adulteries" (14:8).*

The second angel proclaims that the city of Babylon is dust and ashes! In writing of the fall of Babylon, John was probably announcing the coming fall of the Roman empire. But the larger implication of this announcement is the end of the idolatrous world, the world which has turned away from the adoration of God and established the worship of the beast. The angel declares the end of the enemy of the Church—the world which has been at enmity with the people of God.

The angel charges that the people of earth drank "maddening wine" from the center of pagan corruption. This drink caused them to turn away foolishly from the truth. They invited the wrath of God because their life-style became hedonistic and their goals were secular.

> *A third angel followed them and said in a loud voice: "If anyone worships the beast and his image and receives his mark on the forehead or on the hand, he, too, will drink of the wine of God's fury, which has been poured full strength into the cup of his wrath. He will be tormented with burning sulfur in the presence of the holy angels and of the Lamb. And the smoke of their torment rises for ever and ever. There is no rest day or night for those who worship the beast and his image, or for anyone who receives the mark of his name" (14:9-11).*

Those who refuse the mark of the beast will die a martyr's death, but those who bear the mark of the beast will receive a fate worse than death. They will experience the second death and be tormented for ever and ever. There is no reprieve from the eternal consequences of "burning sulfur." Whatever the interpretation of hellfire, the image speaks of agony, restlessness and continuous vexation.

The consequences of judgment arise from the holiness of God. They are the result not of an angry flareup, but of the fact that holiness will not tolerate the presence of evil.

The message for the Church is clear: Choose temporary death by the beast rather than eternal death with the beast.

> *This calls for patient endurance on the part of the saints who obey God's commandments and remain faithful to Jesus. Then I heard a voice from heaven say, "Write: Blessed are the dead who die in the Lord from now on." "Yes," says the Spirit, "they will rest from their labor, for their deeds will follow them" (14:12,13).*

Until the end of the world, there is no other message for the Church than to endure, persevere and be patient. However, endurance does not mean passive resignation, but active resistance to evil. We are to keep the commandments—love God and our neighbor—and remain constant to the teaching and the person of Jesus.

There may be serious consequences for remaining faithful. We may die as martyrs. But even then, we are assured of the Lord's blessing. We are blessed in death by the Lord. And this blessing is not for a special few who will die in the future, but for all who trust in the living Lord even now. The original text could be read, "Blessed *from the moment of their death* are those who die in the Lord."

Their works follow them. Works are the result of faith, and they will not be forgotten, even though we do not earn a place in heaven through our works of goodness. The reward of the righteous is rest now and peace forever—peace and security.

And the Spirit adds, "Yes, indeed." Amen—so be it.

The Harvest

> *I looked, and there before me was a white cloud, and seated on the cloud was one "like a son of man" with a crown of gold on his head and a sharp sickle in his hand. Then another angel came out of the temple and called in a loud voice to him who was sitting on the cloud, "Take your sickle and reap, because the time to reap has come, for the harvest of the earth is ripe." So he who was seated on the cloud swung his sickle over the earth, and the earth was harvested. (14:14-16).*

The Son of man on the white cloud is none other than Jesus. (The phrase, "like a son of man," is a quote from Daniel 7:13.) He now applies the sickle of judgment to the ripe harvest on earth. The Lord is in charge, not the dragon or the beast. It is His world, and He is in control.

In the Old Testament, the cloud signaled the authoritative presence of God. After the Israelites were delivered from Egypt, the cloud guided them through the wilderness. In the book of Revelation, the cloud continues to express divine authority.

The angel brings a message from the Father, who resides in "the temple." This message indicates that the Father is in full agreement for the harvesting to begin.

The first harvest (presumably of grain) is followed by the harvest of grapes:

> *Another angel came out of the temple in heaven, and he too had a sharp sickle. Still another angel, who had charge of the fire, came from the altar and called in a loud voice to him who had the sharp sickle, "Take your sharp sickle and gather the clusters of grapes from the earth's vine, because its grapes are ripe." The angel swung his sickle on the earth, gathered its grapes and threw them into the great winepress of God's wrath. They were trampled in the winepress outside the city, and blood flowed out of the press, rising as high as the horses' bridles for a distance of 1,600 stadia. (14:17-20).*

According to the parables of Jesus, at the end of the world the angels will do the harvesting, although the Lord will remain in charge and initiate the judgment (see Matt 13:41,49).

The judgment takes place "outside the city." If the city represents Jerusalem where the faithful reside, then those outside the holy city are the heathen world, which receives the judgment of God.

Wine from the winepress flows red, like blood. And this blood gushes a distance of 1,600 stadia, or 184 miles, the length of the land of Israel! For that entire great distance, the blood rises as high as the bridles on horses.

The picture is monstrous—impossible!

We have here an example of good old Jewish exaggeration to make a point. (Can a camel actually squeeze through the eye of a needle?) But the meaning is obvious. There will be great carnage, a terrible loss of life. Babylon is fallen, the world subdued. The holy judgment of God finally ends the pagan rule on earth.

Let the Church be forewarned. Let the faithful be prepared. Let all Christians remain faithful to the Lamb!

Questions for Discussion and Meditation

1. In what ways do you see "the beast" in the world's values and goals today?

2. How can we know whether something is of the world or of God? How can we be sure and avoid confusion?

3. How can Christians resist the pressures of society?

4. How does Revelation 14 help us to live in a hostile world?

CHAPTER TEN

The Seven Bowls

Revelation 15 and 16

Get ready for anything, because anything is going to happen! Seven angels are poised to pour out the seven last plagues. This brief chapter is a prologue to the action.

The Seven Angels

I saw in heaven another great and marvelous sign: seven angels with the seven last plagues—last, because with them God's wrath is completed. And I saw what looked like a sea of glass mixed with fire and, standing beside the sea, those who had been victorious over the beast and his image and over the number of his name. They held harps given them by God and sang the song of Moses the servant of God and the song of the Lamb:

"Great and marvelous are your deeds,
    Lord God Almighty.
Just and true are your ways,
    King of the ages.

Who will not fear you, O Lord,
    And bring glory to your name?
For you alone are holy
All nations will come
    and worship before you,
For your righteous acts have been revealed"
(15:1-4).

The last plagues are about to come. They will complete the period of judgment on earth.

But first, we're accorded a vision of the sea of glass mixed with fire. The sea of glass, representing the holiness of God, is the place of origin for the judgment, while the fire indicates the judgment itself. This image emphasizes the point that *judgment is of God,* that it proceeds from His holiness. Since God is holy and righteous, there must be a judgment which brings an end to human wickedness and sin.

The saints are present in heaven. They are with God. They have made it through, like Israel of old delivered through the Red Sea. They have overcome the world because they were true and faithful to Jesus Christ, refusing to worship the beast or his henchmen. That is why they are now rewarded in the presence of the Lamb.

The song of Moses is a song of victory, sung after Israel's deliverance from the Egyptians through the parted sea (see Exod. 15:1-18). It was a celebration of God's salvation, not of the death of the Egyptians. The song of Moses and the song of the Lamb have this in common—they are songs of redemption, of victory over the world, of rescue from the attacks of a powerful and dangerous enemy.

The song glorifies the holy, sovereign God. He is the Creator of all, the Redeemer, the Almighty. The redeemed from every nation of the world will worship the living Lord. Even though all the nations of the world will be led astray by the beast and the false prophet, out of all nations will come those who will join in the worship of the living God! This is the victory of faith. This is the hope of the Christian.

> *After this I looked and in heaven the temple, that is, the tabernacle of the Testimony, was opened. Out of the temple came the seven angels with the seven plagues (15:5,6) .*

John has just referred to the song of Moses. It is natural for him to follow it with a comment about the Tabernacle in the wilderness. The Tabernacle was built under Moses' leadership as a place where God and man would meet. The open temple in heaven, like the Tabernacle in the wilderness, signified the presence of God. It is from the temple, that is from God Himself, that judgment proceeds. Seven angels emerge from that temple.

> *They were dressed in clean, shining linen and wore golden sashes around their chests. Then one of the four living creatures gave to the seven angels seven golden bowls filled with the wrath of God, who lives for ever and ever. And the temple was filled with smoke from the glory of God and from his power, and no one could enter the temple until the seven plagues of the seven angels were completed (15:6-8).*

Carefully, John describes the angels' clothing. Their

appearance conveys royal dignity. They have been prepared for their ominous task. Holy mystery surrounds this final judgment, but once again we are assured that the judgment proceeds from the Lord who is still on the throne of the universe!

Smoke sometimes obscures the glory and power of God, as clouds may hide the sun. But smoke can also express His power and the glory—as it does here. This is one more indication that God is very much present; He is fully in control. The world can only await His final judgment.

The Church needs to hold onto this revelation! God is still in charge, even as "the cup of his wrath" is poured out. (Isa. 51:17) As long as the judgment takes place, no one is able to enter the smoke-filled temple. The closing of the temple doors indicates that judgment is serious business. God does not take it lightly that He must punish the wicked.

The Seven Plagues

Then I heard a loud voice from the temple saying to the seven angels, "Go, pour out the seven bowls of God's wrath on the earth" (16:1).

The vision unfolds, and a loud voice calls attention to God's action. Everyone is able to hear. The bowls are to be poured out, quickly. The judgments come in rapid succession. No intermission is scheduled between the sixth and seventh plagues, as there was during the seals and trumpets.

Parallels abound between the trumpet judgments and the bowl judgments. They are both inflicted on the elements, and people suffer similar ordeals. The trumpets and bowls also bear a resemblance to the plagues in Egypt. But the bowls are more intense, more devastating, more all-encompassing. This is the final act of the wrath of God.

The first angel went and poured out his bowl on the land, and ugly and painful sores broke out on the people who had the mark of the beast and worshiped his image. The second angel poured out his bowl on the sea, and it turned into blood like that of a dead man, and every living thing in the sea died (16:2-3).

The first plague afflicts the land—or, more specifically, people. It falls on all those who belong to the pagan culture, those whose goals are secular and whose life-style is materialistic: they have "the mark of the beast." (As the Israelites were spared from the plagues of the Egyptians, apparently Christians are not tormented by this affliction.)

The scourge of boils and sores is described as both ugly and painful. In spite of modern medical technology, there seems to be no quick cure for this sickness!

The second plague strikes the sea, which turns to blood like the Nile in Egypt in the days of Moses. All sea life, including the organisms and vegetation dies. This sweeping imagery is not to be taken verbatim. The pollution is terrible, but we have not reached the end of the world. This is not the final chapter in the book of Revelation.

The third angel poured out his bowl on the rivers and springs of water, and they became blood. Then I heard the angel in charge of the waters say:

"You are just in these judgments,
*   you who are and who were, the Holy One,*
*   because you have so judged;*
for they have shed the blood of your
*   saints and prophets,*
and you have given them blood to
*   drink as they deserve."*

And I heard the altar respond:

"Yes, Lord God Almighty,
true and just are your judgments" (16:4-7).

In the Middle East, water is a precious commodity. John's readers knew that to pollute all the sources of water would be a disaster which would put an end to life.

As this awful plague is poured out on the earth, many questions arise in the minds of John's readers and in our minds. Why does God judge the world? Why does He allow these painful afflictions? Why all this torment; is it really necessary? Why does the judgment go on and on? We have seen the breaking of seals, the blowing of trumpets, and now the pouring out of these bowls? Isn't God a God of love? Has He not revealed Himself in mercy at the Cross? How does the judgment square with the love of God?

As if in answer, the angel speaks in defense of God's action, spelling out the reasons for the judgment. Even the altar gets into the act, affirming God's righteousness.

Why does the altar speak? The altar, the holy place of God's presence, underlines the authority of heaven.

The defense of God's action hinges on both the actions of the human race and the character of God. The angel makes it clear that judgment has come because of what the world has done: "for they have shed the blood of your saints and prophets." Because of the shed blood of the saints, the sea and the rivers are turned to blood: blood for blood. The suffering Church will be justified. The enemies of the Lord will be punished. Justice will be done, and all wrongs will be righted.

The character of God is often the theme of the book of Revelation. God is true, just, holy and good. *Because* God is God, the divine action is the right course, the only course for the holy, sovereign Lord.

Consider the reverse possibility. If God did *not* judge the world, His nonchalance would announce that sin and rebellion do not matter. What if all evil were treated with a shrug of the shoulders? Does God walk away from crime and corruption, from blasphemy and rebellion, from idolatry and injustice—yes, from the crucifixion of His only Son? Does He not care what people do to each other and to Him? Does He not care about anything?

If God does not act, evil is made to look all right! Holiness, righteousness and truth are no big deal. Justice is irrelevant.

If evil is not punishable, evil is just as valuable as the good! Sin is just as necessary as righteousness! If there is no judgment which puts an end to sin, then our sins will not find us out and crime will pay after all.

In such a state of indifference there can be no "moral universe." Without the action of judgment, God can no longer be considered holy, righteous or just; He is reduced to powerlessness and apathy. Without judgment, the nature, person and character of God—everything we believe about justice, truth, holiness and righteousness—is in doubt! Justice is a necessary consequence of faith in the sovereign Lord!

> *The fourth angel poured out his bowl on the sun, and the sun was given power to scorch people with fire. They were seared by the intense heat and they cursed the name of God, who had control over these plagues, but they refused to repent and glorify him (16:8,9).*

In the dusty regions of the Middle East, the weather can be extremely uncomfortable. The fourth plague, therefore, must have also struck a familiar chord with John's readers. The fourth bowl produces an excruciating heat wave, so that walking outside is like stepping into an oven. So scorching is the sun that people curse God. These curses are an acknowledgement of God's power, an acceptance of the fact that God is in charge of the elements. But this acceptance produces no moral change. There is no repentance, no turning to the Lord, no worship. Like Pharaoh in Egypt of old, the people harden their hearts!

The reaction of the natural man during suffering is to blaspheme God. Only the Spirit of God can produce faith and repentance in times of trouble.

> *The fifth angel poured out his bowl on the throne of the beast, and his kingdom was plunged into darkness. Men gnawed their tongues in agony and cursed the God of heaven because of their pains and their sores, but they refused to repent of what they had done (16:10,11).*

"The throne of the beast" is the center of secular government. The Antichrist rules the world "from his throne." Now his demonic nature is revealed. The world is thrust into darkness, which means moral and spiritual chaos. All those who have received "the mark of the beast" are afflicted, rulers and people alike. Despair and distress are universal. But once again the reaction is unchanged. There is no openness to the Spirit, no repentance—only more cursing.

> *The sixth angel poured out his bowl on the great river Euphrates, and its water was dried up to prepare the way for the kings from the East. Then I saw three evil spirits that looked like frogs; they came out of the mouth of the dragon, out of the mouth of the beast and out of the mouth of the false prophet. They are spirits of demons performing miraculous signs, and they go out to the kings of the whole world, to gather them for the battle on the great day of God Almighty (16:12-14).*

Israel had reason to fear the eastern kings. In Old Testament days, first the Assyrians and then the Babylonians had invaded the land! The boundary of the Euphrates provided a measure of safety, but the drying up of the river gives access for a large invasion which will culminate in the last battle—the nations of the world joining in the contest against the Lord.

Evil spirits proceed from the dragon (Satan), the beast from the sea (Antichrist), and the beast from the earth (the false prophet—actually called that for the first time in Revelation). This, again, is the unholy trinity. It is plain that evil proceeds from all three, not just the dragon (Satan). And this evil proceeds from their mouth. That is, it takes the form of speech—words!

The demonic spirits assume the shape of frogs, which had been declared unclean animals in the Old Testament and were considered evil and sinister by the Jews. The imagery indicates that unclean words from worldly leaders lead to demonic "wonders." These "signs" are not of God. Jesus warned us: "False Christs and false prophets will appear and perform great signs and miracles to deceive even the elect—if that were possible" (Matt. 24:24).

The gullible world—but not the people of God—will be deluded by the works of Satan. And this universal deception will cause the nations to gather for the final clash against God.

In the midst of all these evil happenings, the Church receives another word of hope from the Lord:

"Behold, I come like a thief! Blessed is he who stays awake and keeps his clothes with him, so that he may not go naked and be shamefully exposed (16:15).

This is reassurance for Christians that Christ is coming again—soon. He is not expected by the world powers, but believers are to remain alert: "When these things begin to take place, stand up and lift up your heads, because your redemption is drawing near" (Luke 21:28). Knowing that everything will be all right at some point in history helps us during those times when things are not all right.

All that the Lord asks of us is that "we keep our clothes on." We are to remain spiritually awake, trusting fully in Christ, and we will not be ashamed at His coming. (The early Christians knew that prisoners of war were sometimes stripped of their clothes to humiliate and shame them before their victors.)

Then they gathered the kings together to the place that in Hebrew is called Armageddon (16:16).

There are numerous orthodox scholars who follow the identification of the *Scofield Reference Bible* for Armageddon as "the hill and valley of Megiddo, west of Jordan in the plain of Jezreel." This, according to Scofield, is "the appointed place for the beginning of the great battle in which the Lord, at His coming in glory, will deliver the Jewish remnant besieged by the Gentile world powers."[1]

Dr. Scofield does not explain why Armageddon is that particular valley; he simply states categorically that Megiddo is the place. The difficulty is that the Greek text does not substantiate this identification. It is true that in the history of Israel, several battles have raged in the plain of Megiddo, and the Bible records how God fought on the side of Israel in these battles (see Judg. 5:19, 2 Kings 9:27). Thus the theme of God's victory would be reflected by such a reference.

But the difficulty is that Armageddon cannot be positively identified as the Megiddo—or any other specific place. The fact is that it would be physically impossible to gather millions of people into the small valley of Megiddo and participate in a gigantic battle (see Rev. 9:14-16; 16:12)!

Since Israel has been the center of Biblical attention from the days of Abraham through the Hebrew prophets, and since the scene of this final battle is given a Hebrew name, it is reasonable to assume that the ultimate showdown will take place somewhere in the Holy Land. But to be any more specific about the identification of Armaggeddon is to engage in pure speculation.

Robert H. Mounce, in his commentary on Revelation, admits that thus far we have been defeated in "all attempts at a final answer." He adds, "Fortunately geography is not the major concern. Wherever it takes place, [Armaggeddon] is symbolic of the final overthrow of all the forces of evil by the might and power of God."[2] G. R. Beasley-Murray in the *New Century Bible Commentary* (Eerdmans) agrees: "We are not to think in terms of a geographical locality in Israel....The name stands for an event."[3]

I concur with Mounce and Beasley-Murray that the event is more important than the location. Armageddon stands for a happening. Armageddon represents the final rebellion, the last resistance of humanity against God. It epitomizes the complete victory which belongs to God, the overthrow of all secular powers. The actual location is simply a secondary issue.

> *The seventh angel poured out his bowl into the air, and out of the temple came a loud voice from the throne, saying, "It is done!" Then there came flashes of lightning, rumblings, peals of thunder and a severe earthquake. No earthquake like it has ever occurred since man has been on earth, so tremendous was the quake (16:17,18).*

The land, the sea, the rivers, and now the air—all are subject to destruction!

Here is the last of the last. From the temple itself,

that is from God Himself, sounds forth the final "it is finished." Judgment also comes to an end.

And in this climax we witness fireworks like on a Fourth of July celebration—thunder and lightning, an earthquake of gigantic proportions, immense hailstones. Everything comes crashing in on us like the finale of an electrifying symphony.

> *The great city split into three parts, and the cities of the nations collapsed. God remembered Babylon the Great and gave her the cup filled with the wine of the fury of his wrath. Every island fled away and the mountains could not be found. From the sky huge hailstones of about a hundred pounds each fell upon men. And they cursed God on account of the plague of hail, because the plague was so terrible."* (16:19-21)

Babylon is what John speaks about, but Rome is on his mind. The effect of the earthquake is felt in Rome and beyond. In fact this earthquake rattles many world centers. The secular world undergoes the judgment of God. All who are living without God experience the shaking of the earth.

Cities collapse. Buildings crumble. There is complete devastation.

The world drinks the cup of fury and bears the consequences. Islands and mountains are moved. Since islands and mountains often stand for kingdoms and nations (see Isa. 2:1-5), the quake probably signals the end of the pagan culture.

The blight of hailstones, similar to the disaster in Egypt, rings down the final curtain. The incredible size of the hailstones (100 pounds?) is in keeping with the other fantastic pictures of the book of Revelation.

We may have heard stories of hail the size of golf balls or even baseballs, but never 100-pound hailstones! This final scourge is so terrible that it is beyond description. It spreads havoc and destruction.

But even now, the world does not repent. For the third time in this chapter we are told that people curse the Creator and refuse to give Him glory.

Christians need to take this message seriously.

This is the word of the Lord: We are to continue our witness and prayers for the lost, but we must not be surprised if hardened sinners do not repent. Only the Spirit of God can convict and bring about conversion. And even under conviction, repentance is still a choice. All too often, judgment does not seem to change the hearts of people.

Questions for Discussion and Meditation

1. What is the significance of the heavenly vision (Rev.15) before the bowls are poured out?

2. Why is there an emphasis on the justice of God in these chapters?

3. Do you know anyone who reacts positively to suffering? Negatively? What influences our response?

4. If God's judgments produce only cursing and hostility, not repentance, why does God bring judgment?

CHAPTER ELEVEN

The End of the World: The Fall of Babylon

Revelation 17 and 18

And now the secular world is unmasked; we see the naked truth. It is like a prostitute, offering herself for sale to all who will have her. She is not faithful, but fickle. She offers her shoddy wares to satisfy fleshly appetites.

Her pleasures are material, not spiritual; temporal, not eternal. They are a snare and a trap: "Her steps lead straight to the grave" (Prov. 5:5).

Consider these chapters in the light of John's view of the world as expressed in his first epistle. These words illuminate the whole landscape: "Do not love the world or anything in the world. If anyone loves the world, the love of the Father is not in him. For everything in the world—the cravings of sinful man, the lust of his eyes and the boasting of what he has and does—comes not from the Father but from the world. The world and its desires pass away, but the man who does the will of God lives forever" (1 John 2:15-17).

> *One of the seven angels who had the seven bowls*
> *came and said to me, "Come, I will show you the*
> *punishment of the great prostitute, who sits on*
> *many waters. With her the kings of the earth com-*
> *mitted adultery and the inhabitants of the earth were*
> *intoxicated with the wine of her adulteries" (17:1,2).*

Some commentators interpret the prostitute to
whom the kings of the earth give their allegiance as
false or civil religion—like the emperor worship in
Rome. They teach that this woman represents certain
religions, possibly churches uniting by watering
down their doctrines, or heresies purporting to be
Christian.

To me, these interpretation are suspect, since no
powerful competing or pseudo-Christian religion
(outside of emperor worship) existed in John's time. I
believe it is more logical to say that John is referring to
the dominant world system, which for him was the
Roman empire and all it stood for. He warns
Christians not to be taken in by the tempting, deceit-
ful and exceedingly harmful secularism of the surrounding culture.

The prostitute sits "on many waters," which means
many nations and languages have given their loyalty
to the empire (see v. 15). So it will happen in the last
days that many countries will be aligned with this
unholy power.

The form changes but the essence remains. Rome is
no more, but what Rome stood for is part of the secular culture and will be prominent in the last days.

The world system which lures its subjects is based
on evil seduction and promotes the worship of *things*.
The world makes every attempt to entice us away

from God and into its own arms with the lure of personal profit. Not only the kings of the earth, but "ordinary people" as well, are attracted by secular, hedonistic paganism. They are tempted to "sell their souls." They commit spiritual adultery.

> *Then the angel carried me away in the Spirit into a desert. There I saw a woman sitting on a scarlet beast that was covered with blasphemous names, and had seven heads and ten horns. The woman was dressed in purple and scarlet, and was glittering with gold, precious stones and pearls. She held a golden cup in her hand, filled with abominable things and the filth of her adulteries. This title was written on her forehead:*
>
> *Mystery, Babylon the Great,*
> *the Mother of Prostitutes*
> *and of the Abominations of the*
> *Earth (17:3-5)*

We are told clearly that the woman in the desert represents Babylon the Great. The desert itself is desolate, for Babylon is no more. The haunting emptiness where once stood a great empire is an illustration of the barren condition of the world system.

Many cities in ancient times were considered apostate—Tyre, Nineveh and even Jerusalem, but none was despised more than Babylon for her wickedness. And Babylon had fallen; it no longer existed in John's time. The destruction of Babylon, then, serves as a prophecy of what will happen to Rome and to all humanistic governments. This is the swan song for world powers without God—any society which is opposed to God.

The woman sits on a scarlet beast. The woman represents the center of power, the capital (for John, Rome), and the beast is the empire as a whole. In ancient lore, a woman pictured on a beast is symbolically one with the beast. Sometimes in these old tales, the beast turns into a woman!

The seven heads and ten horns belong to the beast. Since in this kind of literature, heads and horns usually stand for rulers and their realms, it is reasonable to assume that these heads and horns represent the countries which offer allegiance to the world empire (see also Rev. 13:1). The complete numbers seven and ten signify the complete allegiance of the nations to the evil empire.

The color of the woman is the same as the color of the beast. Scarlet and purple speak of royalty and riches. The prostitute is expensively dressed. Her jewelry is elaborate and showy. The golden cup she holds in her hands is costly, and the drink it contains is intoxicating, addicting, immoral and corrupting.

The name written on her forehead is for all to see. In spite of her luxurious appearance, she is really nothing more than a common prostitute—corrupt, evil, and vulgar.

I saw that the woman was drunk with the blood of the saints, the blood of those who bore testimony to Jesus (17:6).

When the lure of the world fails to tempt the Christian, the fickle society will persecute the faithful. Christians may pay for their faithfulness with their blood and their lives. We are not offered protection, even though we remain loyal in our testimony to

Jesus. Yet there will be rewards beyond this world, in the presence of God. The message of Revelation is that there is more to life than the prostitute can provide!

The Explanation

> *When I saw her, I was greatly astonished. Then the angel said to me: "Why are you astonished? I will explain to you the mystery of the woman and of the beast she rides, which has the seven heads and ten horns. The beast, which you saw, once was, now is not, and will come up out of the Abyss and go to his destruction. The inhabitants of the earth whose names have not been written in the book of life from the creation of the world will be astonished when they see the beast, because he once was, now is not and yet will come. This calls for a mind with wisdom. The seven heads are seven hills on which the woman sits. They are also seven kings. Five have fallen, one is, the other has not yet come; but when he does come, he must remain for a little while. The beast who once was, and now is not, is an eighth king. He belongs to the seven and is going to his destruction" (17:7-11).*

The mystery of the woman in the desert is now explained, although commentators disagree about the meaning of the explanation! John is told that the seven heads of the beast represent seven hills. This fits in with the interpretation that the woman represents the city of Rome, and the beast on which she rides denotes the Roman empire. John was well aware that the city of Rome was built on seven hills. Most of his first-century readers would also make the identification easily.

The same number (seven) also delineates seven rulers, again a complete number. Commentators have had great difficulty identifying the five rulers who have fallen (died), the one who is and the one who is to come. The number of Caesars does not fit this accounting! What, then, is the meaning of these numbers?

The beast which was, is not and will come again out of the Abyss portrays the last world power. Some teachers believe that the Roman empire will be revived in the last days. Perhaps so, but it is not necessary to force that interpretation. The point is that Babylon will repeat itself. As Babylon stands for Rome, so Rome represents *any* world power without God. Whether this will actually center in the old city of Rome is uncertain.

It is probably better not to associate names with the seven kings and the eighth. Remember, seven is a complete number, so when the seventh ruler has risen and fallen, the time will be fulfilled and the way prepared for the eighth ruler. He will be related to the world system ("he belongs to the seven") and yet he is different from other rulers—unique, embodying evil. This is the Antichrist, the beast we saw rise out of the sea in Revelation 13. This Antichrist epitomizes corruption. His opposition to God is total. He is the final expression of humanism, the number 666. His rule will end in infamy.

At first he will gain power. Then he will lose power. That, in essence, is the message of Revelation 17!

Once again we are reminded that the name of every Christian is recorded in the book of life. This word of assurance is for Christians who put their trust in the Lamb of God! The book of life is prepared from the creation of the world. The Lord knows those who belong to Him. We are also told that these Christians will not be deceived by this secular, materialistic ruler—although they will be "astonished" to see him.

> *"The ten horns you saw are ten kings who have not yet begun to reign, but who for one hour are to share with the beast the exercise of royal authority; for they have but a single purpose among them and will confer power and authority upon the beast. They will wage war upon the Lamb, but the Lamb will defeat them, for he is Lord of lords and King of kings, and his victory will be shared by his followers, called and chosen and faithful"* (17:12-14, NEB).

These ten kings depict nations who give their allegiance to the harlot-city in the last days. It is possible that these kings represent ten actual nations—perhaps from the east (Rev. 9:14-17). It is not necessary that there be exactly ten. Remember, the number ten, like seven, is a total or perfect number. The point is that *the whole world* sets itself against the Lamb. At the end of history, the nations place their weight behind the beast who has cast a spell over the whole earth.

The rule of these nations is extremely short—certainly far less than the forty-two months of tribulation described in Revelation 11! They are accorded one hour. Again, this does not mean a literal sixty seconds; the meaning is that they will have but a short time in the limelight.

The ten nations rally with the beast against the Lamb. How can the meek Lamb even hope to win out against a hideous beast? It sounds incredible. But with God, the foolish things shame the wise and the weak things overcome the strong (see 1 Cor. 1:27).

Jesus Christ—the Lamb—is the Victor because He is risen from the dead. He has ascended to the Father. He is King of kings. All power, glory and majesty, all praise, honor and wisdom belong to the Lamb and not to the beast (see Rev. 5:12).

And there, standing with the Lamb, now and forever, are His own people. They are the called, the chosen, the faithful.

Jesus has called us out of the world and chosen us to be with Him. We are promised the gift of eternal life. All He asks is that we remain loyal to Him. Until His coming, Christians must continue to live in this seductive, pleasure-crazy, materialistic world with steadfastness, courage and devotion.

> Then the angel said to me, "The waters you saw, where the prostitute sits, are peoples, multitudes, nations and languages. The beast and the ten horns you saw will hate the prostitute. They will bring her to ruin and leave her naked; they will eat her flesh and burn her with fire. For God has put it into their hearts to accomplish his purpose by agreeing to give the beast their power to rule, until God's words are fulfilled. The woman you saw is the great city that rules over the kings of the earth" (17:15-18).

This part of the vision is fully explained. The waters are people—nations and their rulers—who first rally around the harlot-city but then turn on her. There is a revolution, unrest in the wicked empire. Evil precipitates its own destruction. The earthly powers germinate the seeds of their own demise.

The garish, gaudily attired prostitute is uncovered. Her nakedness is exposed. Her destruction comes at the hands of her own followers. And it is a terrible end; she is burned and annihilated.

This is the due reward for the harlot-city's ruthless persecution of the saints. God brings judgment because she has tortured the faithful.

All judgment belongs to the purpose of God. His word will be fulfilled. In that word Christians can put their trust. The Church will not have to endure much longer. The harlot and the beast have met their doom. The righteous Lord and not the lurid prostitute is on the throne, and soon the kingdom of God will come in triumph. He who has ears to hear, let him hear and take courage!

The Fall of Babylon

The world system (Babylon, Rome) has been characterized as an unfaithful, wanton prostitute. Now comes the end of this woman of pleasure—the fall of humanism:

After this I saw another angel coming down from heaven. He had great authority, and the earth was illuminated by his splendor (18:1).

From a heavenly perspective the world seems small and insignificant. God displays His power through His mighty angels, who radiate light and authority.

With a mighty voice he shouted:

"Fallen! Fallen is Babylon the Great!
She has become a home for demons

and a haunt for every evil spirit,
a haunt for every unclean and detestable bird.
For all the nations have drunk
the maddening wine of her adulteries.
The kings of the earth committed adultery with her,
and the merchants of the earth grew rich from her
excessive luxuries" (18:2,3).

Another preview of the end! The world has not yet ceased to be, but its demise is a foregone conclusion. Babylon *has* fallen, and its fall prophesies the coming fall of Rome—and of empires to come. The destiny of all profane powers is to "pass away" (1 John 2:17).

As the Old Testament prophets predicted, Babylon has become a haunt for demons (see Isa. 13:19-22). What could be worse than demon possession? And that is the fate of the secular world. Where God is absent, the devil takes over.

The "unclean birds" are sometimes linked with demonic activity. In any case, unclean birds are to be avoided, just like unclean animals and insects in the Old Testament (see Deut. 14:12-18).

The nations of the world and their populations were deceived by the harlot-city and her empire. They subscribed to the temporal hedonism of the carnal culture. They committed spiritual adultery (apostasy from God). They sold their souls. They lived only for pleasure and success, the pursuit of the "almighty" dollar. And therefore they will suffer the same fate she does.

Then I heard another voice from heaven say:

> *"Come out of her, my people,*
> *so that you will not share in her sins,*
> *so that you will not receive any of her plagues;*
> *for her sins are piled up to heaven,*
> *and God has remembered her crimes" (18:4,5).*

Separation from the world—whether physical or ideological—is a constant theme in the Old Testament. God called Abraham to leave his culture. He told Moses to bring the chosen people out of Egypt. He made it clear that Israel was destined to be a holy nation unto the Lord. And through His prophets, He repeatedly warned His people against bowing down to the idols of foreigners.

The message to Christians in the New Testament is similar: "Come out from them [the practices and goals of unbelievers] and be separate, says the Lord" (2 Cor. 6:17). And God still speaks to the Church in "Babylon." The dangers are great. The temptations are strong. And so His word to us is "Come out of her, my people."

Resist the mark of the beast! Do not be enticed by worldly pursuits—pursue different goals! Hold fast to the truth. Follow the Lamb. Do not live for the frail, sick society which is destined for destruction. Instead, serve the Lord who has bought you with His sacrifice on the cross. Yes, *separate* yourselves from the world system, lest you share in its destruction.

The Just Reward for Sin

The harlot-city's fall is inevitable. Sin will have its just reward: "The wages of sin is death" (Rom. 6:23):

"Give back to her as she has given;
pay her back double for what she has done.
Mix her a double portion from her own cup.
Give her as much torture and grief
as the glory and luxury she gave herself.
In her heart she boasts,
`I sit as queen; I am not a widow,
and I will never mourn.'
Therefore in one day her plagues will overtake her:
death, mourning and famine.
She will be consumed by fire,
for mighty is the Lord God who judges her"
(18:6-8).

The judgment is "double" for her sins (compare Isa. 40:2). "Double" does not suggest two judgments for every one sin; that would be excessive and unfair. The meaning is that the world will receive the same amount of judgment as the sin. The double for every sin is like the reverse side of the same coin. The next sentence explains this meaning: "Give her as much torture and grief as the glory and luxury she gave herself."

As we sow, so shall we reap (see Gal. 6:7). The scales balance equally: sin on one side, judgment on the other.

In one day the reign of the harlot-city comes to an end (v. 8). In one hour it's all over (vv. 10,17,19). The repetition underlines the swiftness of the end. It need not be a literal day or hour. The emphasis is on the swiftness of destruction, on the finality of the judgment, on the rapid turnabout—from queen to widow in such a short time!

The sudden events stun the imagination of all who behold the fire, the famine, the death and destruction.

And the message in the fall of the harlot-city is the theme of all Revelation: God is Almighty, and the world is powerless. That is what the Lord wants us to remember as we face the end of the world.

The Lament over the City

When the kings of the earth who committed adultery with her and shared her luxury see the smoke of her burning, they will weep and mourn over her. Terrified at her torment, they will stand far off and cry:

"Woe! Woe, O great city,
O Babylon, city of power!
In one hour your doom has come!" (18:9,10).

Leaders of nations forget their power exists by the mercy of God. Proud nations boast they will last forever. But when judgment falls, there is no escape. Politicians and military leaders can only mourn their losses.

What a fall—from power to powerless, from luxury to ashes. What terror for those leaders who never dreamed anything like this could happen! This turn of events was not in their projected plans. They dreamed of a brighter and better tomorrow, a glorious and ever more prosperous future. The judgment of God came as a total surprise to them.

The merchants of the earth also will weep and mourn for her, because no one any longer buys their cargoes, cargoes of gold and silver, jewels and pearls, cloths of purple and scarlet, silks and fine linens; all kinds of scented woods, ivories, and every sort of thing made of costly woods, bronze, iron, or marble; cinnamon and spice, incense, perfumes and frankincense; wine, oil, flour and wheat, sheep and cattle, horses, chariots, slaves, and the lives of men (18:11-13, NEB).

World leaders are joined by businessmen in mourning the fallen city. Economic disaster has overtaken the world. The stock market has crashed. Investors have lost everything in a day—in an hour. The food lines have started. Wall Street is as empty as an abandoned refrigerator rusting in a junkyard.

The shopping centers have closed; they are as barren as the Sahara desert. Nothing sells any longer, because no one can afford to buy. The economy comes to a rusty halt.

Jewelry, clothing, homes, furniture, perfume, food, livestock, all modes of transportation—everything is finished. And this even applies to the buying and selling of people. In the history of the world there have always been slaves, human beings bought and sold by the powerful. And even today, when outright slavery has been outlawed, exploitation of human beings by commercial interests continues. (The fear of a pink slip—or just the desire for more money—can enslave a person almost as effectively as manacles and chains.) But even this unsavory part of the world of commerce will come to a grinding halt.

They will say, "The fruit you longed for is gone from you. All your riches and splendor have vanished,

never to be recovered." The merchants who sold
these things and gained their wealth from her will
stand far off, terrified at her torment. They will weep
and mourn and cry out:

"Woe! Woe, O great city,
   dressed in fine linen, purple and scarlet
   and glittering with gold, precious
          stones and pearls!
In one hour such great wealth has been brought
       to ruin!" (18:14-17).

What are these business people moaning about?
They are weeping over their material losses. Their
investments are lost. Their money is gone. They do
not sorrow over the suffering of people. They are not
concerned about personal hurt and misery. They are
not lamenting the afflictions of the innocent. All they
can think about is the crash of the stock market and
the loss of their investments!

What a shock! This was not predicted by political
experts or economic analysts. The judgment of God is
an unforeseen event, an intrusion into the world's
dreamy plans.

Every sea captain, and all who travel by ship, the
sailors, and all who earn their living from the sea,
will stand far off. When they see the smoke of her
burning, they will exclaim, "Was there ever a city
like this great city?" They will throw dust on their
heads, and with weeping and mourning cry out:

"Woe! Woe, O great city,

where all who had ships on the sea
became rich through her wealth!
In one hour she has been brought to ruin!"
(18:17-19).

Now those who deal in imports and exports cry over the same spilled milk that caused the leaders and the business people to weep. They are in anguish because of the demise of the proud, stable, economic system in which they have heavily invested. (What emotions would overwhelm us if we saw New York, London, Paris and Moscow suddenly reduced to rubble and ashes? No one would believe it, either!)

"Rejoice over her, O heaven!
Rejoice, saints and apostles and prophets!
God has judged her for the way she treated you."
(18:20)

But how can anyone rejoice at the demise of the world? Is it proper to speak of rejoicing?

Christians can never rejoice over suffering or pain afflicted on others. The reason for our celebration is the end of apostasy and idolatry, of materialism and hedonism, of luxury and indulgence, of life without God.

The Church is glad because the end of the world spells the end of persecution. There will be no more domination by evil powers, no more intimidation by those who run the world. For the Church, the end of the world spells freedom at last!

Summation

Then a mighty angel picked up a boulder the size of a large millstone and threw it into the sea, and said:

"With such violence
    the great city of Babylon will be thrown down,
    never to be found again.
The music of harpists and musicians, flute players
        and trumpeters,
    will never be heard in you again.
No workman of any trade
    will ever be found in you again.
The sound of a millstone
    will never be heard in you again.
The light of a lamp
    will never shine in you again.
The voice of bridegroom and bride
    will never be heard in you again" (18:21-23).

This is a graphic illustration of the end of the harlot-city. A millstone is thrown and buried in the depth of the sea. Like the disappearing stone, the world of pleasure vanishes.

The music industry is gone. Only silence echoes where once sounded the wild drumbeats, the sensual sounds; the downbeat, the upbeat, and the off beat.

Business has folded too. There is no more manufacturing, no more need for labor.

All trust in Wall Street has evaporated. The dollar and all the world currencies have failed.

The lights have gone out! The utility companies have closed down. The night life of Broadway disappears. The movie industry collapses.

There are no more fun times on earth—not even a wedding.

The picture may be overdrawn, but the point is obvious. The judgment of God has fallen on Babylon the great. With these few paint strokes, the portrait is drawn. It's sufficient to tell us that closing time is approaching.

> *"Your merchants were the world's great men.*
>
> *By your magic spell all the nations were led astray. In her was found the blood of prophets and of the saints, and of all who have been killed on the earth"* (18:23-24).

The judgment has fallen not only because of the harlot-city's sins, but also because of her persecution of the Church. Over the centuries, God's chosen people have been captured and slain, martyred and tossed out on the dungheaps of the world. When the world touches the people of God, it tampers with God Himself. There will be no escape from the consequences of these evil deeds.

God is sovereign and holy. God is just and fair.

Those who try to counter the eternal purposes of God will suffer the just rewards for their actions.

Questions for Discussion and Meditation

1. Why is the secular world pictured as a prostitute in this chapter of Revelation?

2. Why does the secular world hold such fascination for many people?

3. Does the mourning of the world over its sudden end lead to the possibility of repentance? Why or why not?

4. Since we know the outcome, how does this influence our lives today? How can we live for that which is eternal?

CHAPTER TWELVE

The Kingdom and the Final Judgment

Revelation 19 and 20

The judgment has fallen on Babylon. Only Armageddon is still to come. Salvation is near. The Lord God omnipotent reigns!

What a scene! We are overwhelmed by the heavenly host's reaction to the end of the world and by the splendor of their worship. We are struck by the power of the Almighty, the Lord who has acted and who will act.

The Hallelujah Chorus

After this, I heard what sounded like the roar of a great multitude in heaven shouting:

"Hallelujah!
Salvation and glory and power belong to our God,
for true and just are his judgments.
He has condemned the great prostitute

who corrupted the earth by her adulteries.
He has avenged on her the blood of his servants."

And again they shouted:
   "Hallelujah!
        The smoke from her goes up for ever
        and ever" (19:1-3).

The fall of the evil empire precipitates the joyous Hallelujah Chorus. "Hallelujah" means "praise to the Lord." Only now in the book of Revelation, at this point in history, do we hear it. And the hallelujah is repeated four times.

The song is far from meditative and quiet. A multitude of believers no one can number unites to shout and sing. A swelling crescendo rises—a great release of joy! The worldly prostitute has come to an end. The Lord is truly triumphant.

When we Christians feel we are isolated and few in number, a minority in the world, we ought to remember we are a multitude. The redeemed of the Lord are an innumerable throng!

The song delights in the righteousness of God. It does not dwell on destruction and horror, but exalts God's power and majesty. What God does is just and good. Whatever is not just and good cannot be of God. Whatever is not true or holy is not of God. When God brings judgment on sin, He proclaims His salvation. His action is not to be questioned, for God is just and righteous in all that He does.

This is the God whom we believe and serve. This is the God revealed to us in Jesus Christ. This is the sovereign Lord of the universe.

The end of "the great prostitute," the harlot-world, will be perpetual destruction: "The smoke from her goes up for ever and ever." This means there will be no resurrection of paganism, no return to the secular. It's all over—*for good.*

The corruption of truth has ended. The deceptions and spiritual adulteries are paid for. The blood of the saints has been avenged. God has vindicated the righteous.

Because our Lord has acted and will act in truth and justice, we can at all times and in all places follow Him with confidence. He will save us. He will keep us. Most significantly, He is Lord of all. Since Jesus Christ is Lord, the world system does not have a chance. The secular is doomed to perish. Only righteousness and truth will prevail. Only the salvation which is of the Lord is eternal.

> *The twenty-four elders and the four living creatures fell down and worshiped God, who was seated on the throne. And they cried:*
>
> *"Amen, Hallelujah!"*
>
> *Then a voice came from the throne, saying:*
>
> *"Praise our God,*
> *all you his servants,*
> *you who fear him,*
> *both small and great!" (19:4,5).*

The twenty-four elders we saw in the first vision of heaven (Rev. 4–5) continue their worship of God.

Remember, they most likely represent believers from both the Old and New Testament times: twelve tribes of Israel plus twelve apostles. The four living creatures who were instrumental in the earlier judgments also join in adoration. All heaven is united in song.

If all the host of heaven are praising God, so ought all Christians who are alive on earth to praise Him! The Church is to celebrate God always, no matter what our circumstances—before tribulation, during tribulation and after the trials are over.

> *Then I heard what sounded like a great multitude, like the roar of rushing waters and like loud peals of thunder, shouting:*
>
> *"Hallelujah!*
> *For our Lord God Almighty reigns.*
> *Let us rejoice and be glad*
> *and give him glory!*
> *For the wedding of the Lamb has come,*
> *and his bride has made herself ready.*
> *Fine linen, bright and clean,*
> *was given her to wear" [Fine linen stands for*
> *the righteous acts of the saints.]" 19:6-8).*

The Hallelujah Chorus can be heard everywhere, reminding us that our Lord reigns and will reign forever. The Church can safely trust the living Lord, who was, and is and is to come. No matter how evil the times, or how difficult the road, we can live by faith.

Until the climax! And now it is here—the wedding of the Lamb, the marriage, the consummation. The Church is presently engaged to the Lord. She is destined to become His bride.

The meaning of a betrothal in Jewish and early Christian times was much more serious than an engagement is today. A betrothal was a binding commitment, a solid pledge, and to break it was unheard of. Our commitment to Jesus Christ is like a Jewish betrothal. It cannot be broken. We are set apart to become the bride of Christ!

This rich imagery echoes a well-established biblical theme. In the Old Testament, especially the prophets, Israel is often spoken of as God's wife or bride—all too often, an unfaithful one (see Isa. 62:5; Jeremiah 3:1; Hosea 1–3). Jesus, in His parables, referred to Himself as a bridegroom (see Matt. 9:15; John 3:29). And Paul, in Ephesians 5, clearly compared the relationship of Christ and the church to a marriage relationship.

The pictures in Revelation are mixed: "The Lamb" takes "a bride"? But the message is clear. The Church must prepare herself for the coming of her Lord, her bridegroom, by clothing herself in righteousness and purity of heart.

The fine, pure linen that represents righteousness is provided for the bride. Salvation is a gift, and our righteousness is not our own: "Righteousness from God comes through faith in Jesus Christ to all who believe" (Rom. 3:22).

> From heaven He came and sought her
> to be His holy bride,
> With His own blood He bought her,
> and for her life He died.[1]

Through His death on the cross, Jesus has granted us salvation by faith. And through the power of His indwelling Spirit, He wants us to live out our faith. As we put belief into action, we will do "the righteous acts of the saints." This is "faith expressing itself through love" (Gal. 5:6). This is the way we prepare ourselves for the coming of the Bridegroom.

> *Then the angel said to me, "Write: `Blessed are those who are invited to the wedding supper of the Lamb!'" And he added, "These are the true words of God." At this I fell at his feet to worship him. But he said to me, "Do not do it! I am a fellow servant with you and with your brothers who hold to the testimony of Jesus. Worship God! For the testimony of Jesus is the spirit of prophecy" (19:9,10).*

There is a blessing for all who are invited to the feast in heaven. This is stated clearly in a beatitude, like the famous Beatitudes found in the Sermon on the Mount. Those Beatitudes affirm that God's favor is showered on the poor in spirit, the peacemakers, the persecuted, the humble, the merciful, the pure in heart. This beatitude adds another dimension: "Happy are those who are invited to the wedding in Heaven!"

A wedding is always followed by a celebration of some sort. We call these receptions. But in biblical days, a "reception" was a wedding supper, and it lasted much longer than receptions do today. The banquet following the solemn ceremonies was often considered the highlight of all the wedding events. It was a time of feasting, joy and celebration. This kind of deeply felt joy, magnified many times, is in store for people of faith. We are invited to the ceremony, the happy feast, the heavenly banquet.

After the beatitude, the truth of the vision is confirmed. We can believe, we are told, because this is the Word of God. As Jesus bore testimony to the truth, so we are to hold fast to the eternal gospel.

John, apparently thinking that the messenger who brings the invitation is the Lord Himself, falls down to worship. He then discovers that the messenger is an angel and that angels are not to be glorified.

Here, and throughout the book of Revelation, the message is clear: Only God the Father, Jesus Christ the Son and the Holy Spirit are to be accorded glory, honor and praise. And glory, honor and praise is to be given with wholehearted devotion and enthusiasm. Hallelujah!

The Coming of the Lord

Then I saw heaven wide open, and there before me was a white horse; and its rider's name was Faithful and True, for he is just in judgement and just in war (19:11, NEB).

Now a white horse appears—clean, pure, the most majestic of animals. On his back is a rider who, we are told, is called Faithful and True.

This is the moment Christians over the ages have waited for—the return of Jesus Christ.

We can freely put our faith in Him; He is faithful.

He can be trusted; He is the Truth.

He is worthy of our commitment; He will execute justice.

We can follow Him wherever He leads.

We are sure of eternal victory, for He is the risen Lord, and He is the Victor!

His eyes are like blazing fire, and on his head are many crowns. He has a name written on him that no one knows but he himself (19:12).

The Rider's eyes, which are like fire, penetrate and purify; they see right through us. Our Lord is the pure and perfect Judge.

The Rider wears "many crowns." Taken literally, of course, this is a ludicrous picture. But taken symbolically, this is a beautiful picture of unlimited power and majesty.

The crowns of the beast were shabby imitations. The crowns of Jesus are real.

The name of the Rider which no one knows will be revealed momentarily. The name represents the inner character of Christ, the relation of the Son to the Father. The name stands for the hidden nature of the God-Man, which the world cannot begin to understand. Christians cannot fathom that nature, either, but we are told the name nevertheless:

He was robed in a garment drenched in blood. He was called the Word of God (19:13, NEB).

"In the beginning was the Word, and the Word was with God, and the Word was God....The Word became flesh and made his dwelling among us" (John 1:1,14). Jesus is the truest expression of God, the Word God has spoken to the world.

The robe is drenched with blood because Jesus comes in judgment. He is treading the winepress (v.

15). The image is taken from the making of wine in biblical times. Grapes were crushed beneath the feet of those who pressed them out. In the process, the juice might splatter their clothing, turning it the color of blood. The image means that Jesus, coming to judge the world, will be victorious over His enemies. It provides us assurance: We know who will win the battle!

> *The armies of heaven were following him, riding on white horses and dressed in fine linen, white and clean (19:14).*

Are there "armies" in heaven? Do they ride on white horses? What is the meaning of this symbolism?

The vision pictures an innumerable throng which supports the victorious Lord: "*Like* a mighty army moves the Church of God . . ."[2] There are no weapons in the hands of these troops! The Church on earth or in heaven does not carry weapons, for "all who draw the sword will die by the sword" (Matt. 26:52). Besides, there is no need for weapons, for victory has already been won.This heavenly host is clothed in dress uniforms—white linen, hardly an appropriate outfit for fighting. Dress uniforms are for parades, not for battles. The Church is redeemed, purified: "They have washed their robes and made them white in the blood of the Lamb" (Rev. 7:14).

> *Out of his mouth comes a sharp sword with which to strike down the nations. "He will rule them with an iron scepter." He treads the winepress of the fury of*

*the wrath of God Almighty. On his robe and on his
thigh he has this name written:*

King of Kings and Lord of Lords (19:15,16).

Jesus proceeds to carry out the sentence of judgment.

The sword proceeds from His mouth, just as it did
in Revelation 1:16. The mouth is not the place where
anyone would normally carry a sword. But this is not
actually a sword. He speaks the Word of God: "The
word of God is...sharper than any double-edged
sword' (Heb. 4:12).

This Word is the only weapon Jesus uses. Although
our Lord is arrayed as one who comes to "make war,"
there follow no description of a battle, no clash of
armies, no portrayal of how the victory is won, no
mention of bloodshed. The Word of the Lord subdues
the enemy. That is all.

It is significant that Jesus Christ gains the victory
alone; He does not use the armies of heaven which
accompany Him. They back Him, but do not seem to
be involved in the conflict. As strange as it may
sound, the conflict is settled by and with the Word of
truth.

Nevertheless, the victory is decisive. Christ reigns
with a solid authority—an iron scepter. All power is
already given to our risen Lord in heaven and on
earth (see Matt. 28:18).

As grapes are crushed in the winepress, so the
enemy is overwhelmed by the power of the Word. No
worldly potentate will be able to resist Jesus Christ.
He is above all kings, dictators and rulers. The
insignia on His robe and on His person proclaims His

absolute authority, His universal majesty, His power and glory: He is King of kings and Lord of lords.

> *And I saw an angel standing in the sun, who cried in a loud voice to all the birds flying in midair, "Come, gather together for the great supper of God, so that you may eat the flesh of kings, generals, and mighty men, of horses and their riders, and the flesh of all people, free and slave, small and great"* (19:17,18).

The angel in the sun is splendid and glorious. He comes with the authority of God and summons the birds of prey to the grizzly scene that will follow the coming war.

Will the outcome be as gory as it sounds? Will the field be strewn with bodies for the birds to feast on? If the contest is won by the Word of God, how can the result be a bloody battlefield?

Many do interpret this scene literally, of course, expecting a final battle with almost universal carnage. However, I prefer to look at this scene as something which is like a surrealistic painting, in which images and shapes, colors and concepts, combine to give a broad but vivid impression and help us feel the reality. Still, the scene is terrifying, macabre, ominous—a consequence of the power of the Word of God.

The birds, many of them likely carrion eaters—unclean and condemned in the Old Testament—act as instruments of judgment. They complete what has turned into a triumphant day for the Lord.

Since Revelation 16 described the kings of the world gathering at Armageddon, it is usually assumed that the battle will be fought at Armageddon. In this chapter, however, the name "Armageddon" is never specifically mentioned. The emphasis is not on *where the battle takes place*, but on *what the outcome will be*. The Lamb will be victorious. Neither the dragon nor any terrifying beast can stop His glorious kingdom.

> *Then I saw the beast and the kings of the earth and their armies gathered together to make war against the rider on the horse and his army. But the beast was captured, and with him the false prophet who had performed the miraculous signs on his behalf. With these signs he had deluded those who had received the mark of the beast and worshiped his image. The two of them were thrown alive into the fiery lake of burning sulfur. The rest of them were killed with the sword that came out of the mouth of the rider on the horse, and all the birds gorged themselves on their flesh (19:19-21).*

Here we see the demise of the beast and all world rulers. We also see the end of the false prophet, who led people down the path of secularism. Their day has been short-lived. Their doom is certain.

All who are deceived by the devil, who give their allegiance to the hedonistic age and reject Jesus Christ as Lord must now suffer the consequences. Those who accept "the mark of the beast" will share the lot of the beast.

The Word of God is the final authority. The Word of God will judge them. Those who choose to be their own salvation will not save themselves. They don't have a chance.

All that remains now is to deal with the dragon who deceived the nations, whose power established the beast, the false prophet and the prostitute. His doom, too, is certain, as we shall discover.

Christians who read this book learn to rejoice. They are guaranteed the victory, not only someday, but today! Revelation contains a preview of the end. We can live in confidence and peace, trusting in the Lord who came back from the dead and knowing that the One we serve is the King of kings and Lord of lords.

The Millennium

The dragon will now meet his doom. When he does, the Lord's victory will be complete:

> *And I saw an angel coming down out of heaven, having the key to the Abyss and holding in his hand a great chain. He seized the dragon, that ancient serpent, who is the devil, or Satan, and bound him for a thousand years. He threw him into the Abyss, and locked and sealed it over him, to keep him from deceiving the nations anymore until the thousand years were ended. After that, he must be set free for a short time (20:1-3).*

Here the identity of the dragon is made explicit. He is the old serpent who enticed Adam and Eve in the garden. He is the tempter who confronted Jesus in the desert. He is the deceiver our Lord unmasked as a liar and murderer (John 8:44).

Now, however, the prophecy of Jesus is fulfilled: "I saw Satan fall like lightning from heaven" (Luke 10:18).

An angel holds the key to the Abyss. This key has been given him by Jesus, who alone has charge of the keys (Rev. 1:18). The angel hurls Satan into the Abyss. There he is chained and kept under lock and key—to make sure he is unable to roam about and deceive the world nor persecute the Church for period of a thousand years (commonly called the Millennium).

But why only a thousand years? Why not forever? Why must Satan be loosed again after the thousand years are completed? Why should the whole circus start all over again?

We are not given a clear answer. But the implication is that God's purposes are not yet fulfilled. The "forever" is not yet; it is still to come (v. 10). In the meantime, however, the world enjoys the Millennium, a reign of peace.

> *I saw thrones on which were seated those who had been given authority to judge. And I saw the souls of those who had been beheaded because of their testimony for Jesus and because of the word of God. They had not worshiped the beast or his image and had not received his mark on their foreheads or their hands (20:4).*

The thrones are for Christians. They share in the reign of Christ (see Rev. 2:26).

Martyrs are singled out for special mention. They were faithful to the Lord and to the Word of God, even when such faithfulness meant death. It is impossible to live counter to the world without paying a price. But whatever the price, Christians will "come to life" and "reign with Christ"! Those who resist the pressures and temptations of the secular world around us will be eternally with the Lord. These promises encourage us to be followers of the Lamb, today.

> *They came to life and reigned with Christ a thousand years. (The rest of the dead did not come to life until the thousand years were ended.) This is the first resurrection. Blessed and holy are those who have part in the first resurrection. The second death has no power over them, but they will be priests of God and of Christ and will reign with him for a thousand years (20:4-6).*

There are two deaths and two resurrections. Those who take part in the first resurrection will not experience the second death. For those who participate in the second resurrection, there will be those who will undergo what is called "the second death"—eternal separation from God (v. 14).

The first resurrection takes place before the Millennium; the second takes place after it. The saints who rise in the first resurrection reign with Christ during the thousand years. The apostle Paul also describes this first resurrection: "The Lord himself will come down from heaven... and the dead in Christ will rise first. After that, we who are still alive and are left will be caught up together with them in the clouds to meet the Lord in the air. And so we will be with the Lord forever" (1 Thess. 4:16,17).

The first resurrection is selective. The second is universal: "All who are in their graves will hear his voice and come out—those who have done good will rise to live, and those who have done evil will rise to be condemned" (John 5:28,29). The two resurrections are of a different nature and are separated by a thousand years.

God has made those who participate in the first resurrection both kings and priests (Rev. 1:6). This
promise is fulfilled when all who are raised from the
dead serve with Christ on earth. This, in fact, seems to
be one of the purposes of the Millennium—to reward
the faithful, especially martyrs, a chance to reign
along with Christ.

It is important to note that there are differences
between the Kingdom described here—the reign of
Christ on earth—and the new heaven and the new
earth which follow (Rev. 21,22). Sin still exists in the
Kingdom, but not in the new heaven and earth. When
Satan gets one more chance to deceive the world, after
his thousand year's confinement, he is successful. He
gains a large following!

But how are we to understand "the Millennium"?
Will there actually be such a thousand-year reign on
earth?

The kingdom of God prophesied in the Old
Testament was never limited to a thousand-year period; it was to be "forever." The promise of the eternal
Kingdom was repeated at the birth of Jesus: "The
Lord God will give him the throne of his father David,
and he will reign over the house of Jacob forever; his
kingdom will never end" (Luke 1:32,33). And
although Jesus announced that the kingdom of God
was "at hand," He never specified a particular period
of time.

Christians have wrestled with the question of the
Millennium since the apostolic age. Its meaning has
been interpreted in a variety of ways. From the second century on, many scholars taught that they were
actually living during the time of the Millennium.
Augustine, for example, believed the thousand-year

period had begun with Jesus and would extend until His return—possibly around A.D.1000. The Reformers in the sixteenth century taught that the Millennium started under Constantine, who declared Christianity the official religion of Rome and brought the persecution of the Church to a halt. According to the Reformers, the golden age ended with the rise of the Turks and the Moslem invasion of the West.

Few Christians today accept such historical interpretations—especially as more and more time has elapsed since the beginning of the Christian Era. But commentators are still widely divided as to how the thousand years are to be interpreted.

Some scholars do not believe in a literal thousand years' reign at all. They affirm (as I have elsewhere in this book) that numbers in Revelation are figurative: for example, three stands for the trinity, six for man, seven for God. Ten is a complete number and one thousand—ten times ten—means perfection. If 144,000 represents twelve Jewish tribes times twelve apostles multiplied by a thousand to perfection, they say, why should the thousand years be taken literally? To them, the description of the kingdom of God in Revelation signifies *its character*, not *its precise duration*.

This is the position taken by G. R. Beasley-Murray in the *New Century Bible Commentary*: "John's adoption of the figure 1000 for the messianic kingdom is intended to indicate not so much its length as its character, namely as the sabbath of history. Such a view harmonizes with the notion, of importance to John, that creation prefigures new creation, and it links with the idea, attested in Hebrews (ch. 4) of God's sabbath-rest as a type of the kingdom."[3]

Other scholars, however, see the Millennium as a literal period of a thousand years. (Hence the name "Millennium," which refers to a thousand-year period of time.) These scholars stress that the establishment of Christ on the throne during this period fulfills promises in both the Old and New Testaments (2 Sam. 7, Isa. 11, Luke 1:31-33, Acts 1:6,7).

The difficulty with such a literal translation is that Old Testament prophecies of God's coming Kingdom never specify a literal thousand years. In fact, Jewish speculation as to the length of the kingdom of God ranges from 40 to 7000 years! In the literature between the Old and New Testaments (the Apocrypha), Enoch spoke of a messianic kingdom lasting "a week"—corresponding to what he saw as seven weeks of human history (1 Enoch 93; 91:12-17). Some Jewish scholars interpreted such a week as a thousand years, hence 7000. But in 2 Esdras 7:28, the kingdom is said to be only 400 years.

While the apostle Paul does not speak directly of the Millennium, he points to a time when the risen Christ will rule *before* the kingdom is given to God the Father: "Then the end will come, when he hands over the kingdom to God the Father after he has destroyed all dominion, authority and power. For he must reign *until* he [God] has put all his enemies under his feet. The last enemy to be destroyed is death" (1 Cor. 15:24-26, emphasis added). According to this interpretation, the Millennium precedes the death of death (see Rev. 20:14).

I find it very difficult to make a categorical statement about the Millennium. I do believe in the coming kingdom of our Lord. I believe He will reign in power and glory. I look forward to that event in hope.

But whether it will be an actual 1000 year reign is really of little importance to me *now!* What really matters is that I live in light of the promise that Jesus Christ will be triumphant.

Whatever the specific interpretation, the message for Christians is still the same: Live in faith. Be patient. Persevere in the truth. Until the Kingdom arrives, hold to the testimony of Jesus!

The End of Satan

When the thousand years are over, Satan will be released from his prison and will go out to deceive the nations in the four corners of the earth—Gog and Magog—to gather them for battle. In number they are like the sand on the seashore. They marched across the breadth of the earth and surrounded the camp of God's people, the city he loves. But fire came down from heaven and devoured them. And the devil, who deceived them, was thrown into the lake of burning sulfur, where the beast and the false prophet had been thrown. They will be tormented day and night for ever and ever (20:7-10).

Once again, the questions surface. Why is Satan released? Why did the King of the universe not end all possibility of evil? Why did He throw the beast and false prophet, but not the dragon, into the lake of fire? What is the point of another rebellion?

And once again, there are no certain answers—but the release of Satan must be within the purpose of God. Perhaps God wants to tell us something else. Is it that the freeing of Satan underlines the basic defect of human nature—that the world has not changed during the rule of the Lamb? The world has subjected itself to the Lord's rule, but the moment the tempter comes on the scene, the world jumps at the chance to march down the broad road to destruction.

The rebellion is worldwide. It gathers momentum quickly. How suddenly are sinners overtaken by temptation. How deep and damaging are anarchy and revolt in the human heart!

It is clear that imprisonment in the Abyss has not changed Satan. The devil is not about to repent. But Satan does not originate sin! Rather, the tempter tempts the temptable! Sin is in human nature, in our hearts: "From within, out of men's hearts, come evil thoughts, sexual immorality, theft, murder, adultery, greed, malice, deceit...*All these evils* come from inside and make a man `unclean' " (Mark 7:21-23, emphasis added).

The fundamental issue in the world is not social, political or economic. The fundamental problem is the human problem—the problem of sin. This is why Satan has a comparatively easy time of bewitching the world, even after the thousand years of peace!

But the people of God are not fooled; they remain true to the Word. Although the secular world surrounds and swarms about "the camp of God's people," the faithful are not misled by the demonic. The Church perseveres in the love of God.

Then God acts once again. He defends "the camp of God's people," and He gains the last victory. The Church does not have the power to defeat the enemy. That power belongs to God alone.

Now it's all over—finally. The devil is thrown into

the lake of fire—doomed to be confined there forever and ever. There will be no more reprieves, no more chances for the same old scenario. He has been cast out of heaven and now from the earth.

The Great White Throne

> *Then I saw a great white throne, and the One who sat upon it; from his presence earth and heaven vanished away, and no place was left for them (20:11, NEB).*

This vision is awesome indeed! The throne which caught John's attention in the earlier vision (Rev. 4-5) now dominates the scene. It is majestic and glorious, gleaming white in holiness and purity. The judgment proceeds, and the justice is complete. There are no gray areas. The righteous, compassionate Judge is on the throne, the only One worthy to judge.

The scene is overpowering. Even the land and sky flee from the majesty and greatness of God. Jesus predicted that the "earth will pass away" (Matt. 24:35), now this prediction is fulfilled. In the presence of God's glory and power, all sin and that which belongs to earth disappears.

The Judge is on the throne. Most people assume that this Judge is God the Father, but all judgment has been accorded to the Son. The triune God—Father, Son and Holy Spirit—will judge us. Jesus affirmed that all responsibility for judgment had been given to Him. He entered the world and took on human flesh. He is able to identify with human weakness and temptation. We will have no excuses, since "the Son of man" has lived among us. "The Father judges no one, but has entrusted all judgment to the Son" (John 5:22).

> *And I saw the dead, great and small, standing before the throne, and books were opened. Another book was opened, which is the book of life. The dead were judged according to what they had done as recorded in the books. The sea gave up the dead that were in it, and death and Hades gave up the dead that were in them, and each person was judged according to what he had done (20:12-13).*

All will be judged. No one will be overlooked. The final judgment extends to everyone who has ever lived—great and small. It draws people from earth and sea, from the grave and Hades, from all places of the dead. These details assure us that the judgment will be complete. No one will escape the great white throne!

The idea of a divine register—a book of life—goes back to the days of Moses. Moses pleaded with God to "blot him out of the book of life." He was willing to suffer the consequences in order that the people of God may be forgiven for their sin (Exod. 32:32). The prophet Isaiah speaks of those who have been recorded for life in Jerusalem (Isa. 4:3). Daniel linked the book with the judgment (Dan. 12:1).

Does God keep books on us? Are there records in heaven? Or is this a metaphorical way of illustrating what we can readily understand? On earth we keep books on everything. We keep records not only in courts of law, but in business and government, in every field of human endeavor—even in church. Record keeping is a way of keeping track of what is valuable, of maintaining order and accountability. I believe it is reasonable to see the book of life in this way—as a symbol that we are valuable to God, that He is in control, and that we are accountable for the way we live our lives.

Jesus told His disciples, "Rejoice that your names are written in heaven" (Luke 10:20). Is your name recorded in the book?

> *Then death and Hades were thrown into the lake of fire. The lake of fire is the second death. If anyone's name was not found written in the book of life, he was thrown into the lake of fire (20:14,15).*

The second death spells the end of sin and death. With the defeat of death the result of death, Hades, is terminated. The lake of fire marks the conclusion of resistance and rebellion, of evil and deception, of lust and selfishness.

The verdict which decides between the second death and eternal life is based on works, which are the irrefutable evidence of faith (James 2:26). Without the righteous action of the saints, there will be no rewards (Rev. 19:8). Faith which does not transform itself into loving action is not genuine, living faith.

This picture of the judgment is consistent with Paul's teaching in Romans 2:12-16. People will be judged according to how they have lived. The question is not whether they have known the law of God, but whether they have lived according to the law. If they have not heard of God's law, the question becomes whether they did "by nature things required by the law?" (Rom. 2:14). The judgment of God is a judgment of the secrets of the human heart (see Rom. 2:16), for it is out of the heart that life, good or bad, proceeds (see Luke 6:43-45).

Stark alternatives:
Life or death. Heaven or hell.
The end of darkness. Light triumphant.
The end of evil. Reigning righteousness.
The end of rebellion. The completion of justice.

God is sovereign. God is in control. Everything is made clear.

God has been standing in the wings, waiting to come on stage! He has been present, waiting during the tribulation of Christians in the world. Now the King of kings has arrived. The evil empire is finished. The enemies of God—even death and Hades and the devil—are destroyed The victory belongs to the risen Lord. And He will reign forever and ever.

Hallelujah!

All's well that ends well.

Questions for Discussion and Meditation

1. What is new about the Rider on the white horse which we have not previously read in the book of Revelation?

2. Although the language sounds military, what does the coming of Christ describe?

3. Why is Satan locked up for a thousand years, only to be let loose again? What is the point?

4. "In hell no one takes an interest in you" (Ernest Becker). How would you describe hell?

5. If this were the last day of your life, how would you spend it?

CHAPTER THIRTEEN

The New Heaven and Earth

Revelation 21 and 22

The conclusion of the book of Revelation is certainly not disappointing! There is no question mark, no uncertainty, no indecision about the end. God will achieve His eternal purpose. The ideal will become open reality. Every Christian's hope and longing will be actualized. Everything will be created anew.

> *Then I saw a new heaven and a new earth, for the first heaven and the first earth had passed away, and there was no longer any sea. I saw the Holy City, the new Jerusalem, coming down out of heaven from God, prepared as a bride beautifully dressed for her husband (21:1,2).*

God is the God of new beginnings, not of endings. He makes all things *new.*

God is the God of the new heaven and earth, not of the old world of sin.

God is the God of joy and life, of celebration and glory.

In the new creation there will be no oceans. For the Israelites, never a seafaring people, the waters of the sea symbolized danger and evil. Remember, the first beast (representing the secular, materialistic world) arose from the sea. With the elimination of the sea, there is nothing to fear in the new creation.

The holy city which descends from heaven depicts the saints. It is not a city in the sense of streets and buildings, since it is identified as the bride of Christ. This city consists of people, just as the Church consists of people. And this holy congregation, as the bride of Christ, has been in the process of preparing herself for the wedding (Rev. 19:7).

Christians have been raised from the dead. With Christ, they enter the new heaven and earth. They have received life from above. Their perfection is not a human achievement. Holiness, righteousness and salvation are of God, not of the flesh. Having received complete redemption, they are now truly "saints."

As the holy city descends, we are introduced to a new heaven and earth. But why do we need *earth*, if we have heaven? If we live eternally in heaven, what is the purpose of a new earth?

The reason is that heaven and earth are considered one. They were originally created as an entity: "In the beginning God created the heavens and the earth" (Gen. 1:1). Sin entered the world and alienated the earth from God. With the judgment of God, however, evil has been penalized and removed. Earth can now be recreated and heaven and earth be perfectly united once more.

The Greeks and Egyptians, among many other peoples, believed that the soul leaves the body and goes to a separate spiritual heaven. The Jews, on the other hand, placed the kingdom of God on earth. (Some even held the doctrine of the resurrection of the body.)

Heaven typifies a spiritual resurrection, earth a physical resurrection. Heaven is spirit; earth is body. And the union of heaven and earth is like a marriage of the physical and the spiritual. All is made new; all is perfected and redeemed.

> *I heard a loud voice proclaiming from the throne: "Now at last God has his dwelling among men! He will dwell among them, and they shall be his people, and God himself shall be with them. He will wipe every tear from their eyes; there shall be an end to death, and to mourning and crying and pain; for the old order has passed away" (21:3,4, NEB).*

In times past, God made His presence real to His people. He guided His chosen people, Israel, through the wilderness. His glory filled the temple of Solomon. He appeared in the form of a dove to bless Jesus' baptism, and He manifested Himself as tongues of fire at Pentecost.

Those special appearances were unforgettable, but temporary. In the new heaven and new earth, the temporary has turned into the eternal. God and the people of God are brought together for ever and ever. God is present with us. He reveals His glory. All things have become new.

Pain, suffering and sorrow are no more. Sin is gone. Evil is eliminated. The consequences of evil are removed. Hades and death, the last enemy, are destroyed. All that is not of God is extracted from our thought and existence. All that is of God becomes our reality and truth. What freedom, what joy, what grace, what peace, what glory!

We cannot fully anticipate perfection while we are imperfect. We are like children not yet grown and mature: "When perfection comes, the imperfect disappears. When I was a child, I talked like a child, I thought like a child, I reasoned like a child. When I became a man, I put childish ways behind me" (1 Cor. 13:10-11).

The Christian life begins with salvation and ends in salvation.

The Lord and the New

> *He who was seated on the throne said, "I am making everything new!" Then he said, "Write this down, for these words are trustworthy and true." He said to me, "It is done. I am the Alpha and the Omega, the Beginning and the End" (21:5,6).*

This is a certain affirmation that the Revelation is true. The vision can be trusted. The Lord God adds His signature to the prophecy.

God acts. God is in control. God is the sovereign Lord. God has been on the throne of the universe throughout history. The Church has lived by faith in the risen Lord. Now faith is realized; His eternal purpose accomplished.

Human beings cannot bring in the golden age. Human beings may have dreams, but they are unable to fulfill those dreams through science, philosophy, education, government, sociology, economics, or any other human endeavor. The new heaven and new earth are the product of the one and only Creator.

He is the Alpha and Omega. He was present at the beginning. He is here at the end of history. And He will be present for all eternity.

> *"To him who is thirsty I will give to drink without cost from the spring of the water of life. He who overcomes will inherit all this, and I will be his God and he will be my son. But the cowardly, the unbelieving, the vile, the murderers, the sexually immoral, those who practice magic arts, the idolaters and all liars—their place will be in the fiery lake of burning sulfur. This is the second death"* (21:6,7,8).

Jesus Christ invites the thirsty to come and drink from the water of life (see John 7:37). The "drink of eternity" is free (see Isa. 55:1) for the asking. This is the expectation we can have for eternity: our needs will be completely satisfied forever.

Once more, Jesus Christ encourages us to persevere in our trials. He reminds us that the rewards will be great for those who overcome the world. He also reminds us that Christians are members of the family of God and will inherit all things. As children of God, we become brothers and sisters of one another: "If we are [God's] children, then we are heirs—heirs of God and co-heirs with Christ, if indeed we share in his sufferings in order that we may also share in his glory" (Rom. 8:17).

But who are those who do not belong to the eternal family of God? Who are those who undergo "the second death"? Why do they miss out on the marriage and the festivities of life?

They are the cowardly—those who fear "the beast"

more than they fear God. They are unbelievers who do not trust the Lamb. Instead, they serve secular materialism, pleasure and profit; self instead of Christ. They succumb to the pressures of the crowd—"everybody does it." They disregard all standards of decency. They seek personal power any way they can. This is why they lose life!

They are the evil, the deceived, the worldly, the apathetic. They turn from the truth to worship and serve the lie. They miss the target and stray wide of the mark.

The judgment exterminates all evil. It stands like an invincible wall between the old and the new. Nothing foreign to the glory of God and His holiness can penetrate the wall. The new heaven and earth are righteous, redeemed and actually *pure.*

The New Jerusalem

> *One of the seven angels who had the seven bowls full of the seven last plagues came and said to me, "Come, I will show you the bride, the wife of the Lamb." And he carried me away in the Spirit to a mountain great and high, and showed me the Holy City, Jerusalem, coming down out of heaven from God (21:9,10).*

The closing chapters of Revelation have sometimes been called "the tale of two cities." What a contrast between the city of man and the city of God: Babylon and Jerusalem, Rome and the holy city, the prostitute and the bride, the deceiving harlot and the wife of the Lord, the secular and the sacred, the idolatrous and the faithful!

The new Jerusalem is called the bride and the wife of Christ in the same breath. The words suggest no waiting period between. For the Jews a fiancee is considered a bride from the time of her betrothal! The commitment is that serious, the bond that strong. Once betrothed, she is to devote most of her time to preparing for the wedding. We, too, are betrothed—destined to be the bride of Christ; that places a new dimension on faith.

The happy vision of the eternal city gives us hope and promise. We are to live by that hope until our hope is realized.

Both the bride and the city emphasize the fact that, although we are saved individually, we live eternally in community and fellowship. There is *one* bride of Christ, *one* city made up of the redeemed.

The fact that the city comes down from heaven underlines that salvation is by the grace of God.

> *It shone with the glory of God, and its brilliance was like that of a very precious jewel, like a jasper, clear as crystal. It had a great, high wall with twelve gates, and with twelve angels at the gates. On the gates were written names of the twelve tribes of Israel. There were three gates on the east, three on the north, three on the south and three on the west. The wall of the city had twelve foundations, and on them were the names of the twelve apostles of the Lamb (21:11-14).*

Some commentators take the description of the holy city literally—believing that Revelation gives a picture of the future dwelling place of the redeemed. I prefer to interpret the city of God, like the bride of Christ, as the people of God.

The comparison of the city to a precious jewel communicates its perfection, purity and splendor. Surely it is not necessary to think in terms of real stones! The picturesque language describes the glory of God among the redeemed and the perfection and glorification of the saints (see Rom. 8:30). The vision of the holy city is a spiritual truth. If we attempt to take it literally, we will end up scratching our heads and wondering what is going on here. But if we look at the holy city as the bride of Christ and the community of redeemed believers, not a glittering, bejewelled town of fantastic proportions, we catch a glimpse of the wonder of life in the new heaven and new earth..

The walls stand for protection. Ancient cities constructed walls for safety, to guard them from the enemy. But why does the city of God need protection? The dragon and the beast are in the lake of fire, and only the holy and the good dwell in the new heaven and earth. The wall, therefore, does not wall anything out, nor does it wall us in. It simply underlines our security in Christ.

Gates speak of entry—of freedom. The redeemed of the Lord are free to come and go as they please.

Who lives in this city? The followers of the Lamb. They include those from the twelve tribes of Israel, the chosen people of the Old Covenant, who "are of the faith of Abraham" (Rom. 4:16).

The twelve apostles of the Lamb form the foundation. They personify the chosen people of the New Covenant. The Church rests on the foundation of the apostles and prophets (see Eph. 2:20).

Note the repetition of the number twelve. The twelve tribes constitute Israel; the twelve apostles formed the nucleus for the new Israel. The holy city is made up of Jewish believers and Christians, the old covenant and the new. Christ "himself is our peace, who has made the two one and has destroyed the barrier, the dividing wall of hostility" (Eph. 2:14). By His death, He has opened the way for all to be one. Distinctions of race, sex and status have been removed (see Gal. 3:28).

> *The angel who talked with me had a measuring rod of gold to measure the city, its gates and its walls. The city was laid out like a square, as long as it was wide. He measured the city with the rod and found it to be 12,000 stadia in length, and as wide and high as it is long. He measured its wall and it was 144 cubits thick, by man's measurement, which the angel was using (21:15-17).*

The measurement of the city emphasizes its flawlessness. A square contains perfectly equal sides. A cube stretches perfection to perfection. The holy of holies in the temple at Jerusalem was also in the form of a cube (see 1 Kings 6:20).

A cube has twelve edges (lines where the faces of the cube intersect). Twelve multiplied by 12,000 stadia is 144,000. We are familiar with that number in Revelation. The square of each edge—the surface area of one of the faces of the cube—turns out to be 144. These calculations emphasize the unity (one cube) between Jewish and Christian believers (12 x 12).

But let's get to the issue. Twelve thousand stadia equals 1500 miles. Is it possible to conceive of a city 1500 miles long and 1500 miles wide? What about a city 1500 miles wide and long and 1500 miles *high?* What would be the point?

Surely these measurements are symbolic! They point to the perfection of God's people. The city of God is so enormous that the people of God extend "from earth to heaven."

The walls measure 144 cubits, which is 200 feet. Some interpret the walls to be 200 feet thick! Others consider 200 feet to be its height. But what good would a 200-foot wall accomplish around a 1500-mile-high city? The more questions we ask, the more obvious it seems to me that these numbers cannot be taken at face value.

I believe it is important to bring this same reasoning to the following imagery:

> *The wall was made of jasper, and the city of pure gold, as pure as glass. The foundations of the city walls were decorated with every kind of precious stone. The first foundation was jasper, the second sapphire, the third chalcedony, the fourth emerald, the fifth sardonyx, the sixth carnelian, the seventh chrysolite, the eighth beryl, the ninth topaz, the tenth chrysoprase, the eleventh jacinth, and the twelfth amethyst. The twelve gates were twelve pearls, each gate made of a single pearl. The great street of the city was of pure gold, like transparent glass (21:18-21).*

Once again we have a vision of purity, perfection, indescribable beauty, majesty, splendor, excellence, glory. The city specified here is magnificent beyond description.

Once again, there is no need to be literal. The precious stones emphasize the enduring quality of the city of God.

The cheap glitter of Babylon, the city of flesh, has passed away. The economy which created false riches has collapsed. The gross, material world is no more. The worldly city has turned into dust and ashes, but the city of God shines in eternal brilliance.

Gates of pearl (each gate a single pearl, and big enough to fit a two-hundred-foot wall)! Streets of gold (transparent as glass). The familiar description need not evoke actual jewels and solid nuggets. Rather, the beautiful imagery speaks of the ultimate in grandeur, splendor, value, magnificence and majesty. This is the holy city of God.

> *I did not see a temple in the city, because the Lord God Almighty and the Lamb are its temple. The city does not need the sun or the moon to shine on it, for the glory of God gives it light, and the Lamb is its lamp. The nations will walk by its light, and the kings of the earth will bring their splendor into it. On no day will its gates ever be shut, for there will be no night there. The glory and honor of the nations will be brought into it. Nothing impure will ever enter it, nor will anyone who does what is shameful or deceitful, but only those whose names are written in the Lamb's book of life (21:22-27).*

The Body of Christ is like "a spiritual house" (1 Pet. 2:5), a "building...joined together... to become a holy temple"(Eph. 2:21). The Body of Christ is a sanctuary. God is present with His people. This explains why the city is "holy." "The dwelling of God is with men, and he will live with them" (Rev. 21:3) There is no need for another temple when all is temple.

The reason the sun and the moon are not necessary for light is that God is light and "in him there is no darkness at all" (1 John 1:5). The Lamb is the light of the world (John 8:12). Those who follow the Lamb will never dwell in darkness.

From all over the world, from every nation and people, the faithful enter the holy city. Christ died for the world. The potential of redemption from every tribe and country through the preaching of the word encourages the Church to enlarge her vision and take the gospel witness to the ends of the earth!

Clearly, nothing which is impure or harmful will enter the holy city. Only those whose names are recorded in the Lamb's book of life receive eternal life, only those who remain faithful to the Lord in every crisis. Good and evil are forever separated, heaven and hell. This is the great and final divorce.

The River of Life

> *Then the angel showed me the river of the water of life, as clear as crystal, flowing from the throne of God and of the Lamb down the middle of the great street of the city. On each side of the river stood the tree of life, bearing twelve crops of fruit, yielding its fruit every month. And the leaves of the tree are for the healing of the nations (22:1,2).*

The paradise that was lost (Genesis) is now regained (Revelation). The river of life watered the garden of Eden. Now the same river, renewed, courses through the city of God; an unceasing flow of life proceeds directly from God and the Lamb. The water is clear, unmixed, pure.

The tree of life, lost when humans left Eden, is also regained in the new heaven and earth. The fact that a tree of life "stood on each side of the river" could be speaking of more than one tree, perhaps even a row of trees. Maybe it speaks of different fruit trees. The monthly bearing of fruit symbolizes abundance and variety.

Is the fruit actually needed? Do we consume food in the new creation? Who can say? But the implication is clearly that every human need—every requirement for health and joy—is met.

> *No longer will there be any curse. The throne of God and of the Lamb will be in the city, and his servants will serve him. They will see his face, and his name will be on their foreheads. There will be no more night. They will not need the light of a lamp or the light of the sun, for the Lord God will give them light. And they will reign for.ever and ever (22:3-5).*

The curse of Eden—the need to work hard to survive—is removed. Instead, there is blessing—the joy of serving the Lord. Dark, dreaded night is also gone forever, and there is only day, only light. The deeds of the night will cease, and only that which can be brought to the light will exist in eternity. "Everyone who does evil hates the light, and will not come into the light...Whoever lives by the truth comes into the light" (John 3:20,21).

Even more wonderful—we will see the face of God! "Seeing God" was something denied even to the saints on the old earth. But in the new heaven and earth, the glory of God becomes a visible reality! Faith turns into sight. Sin and death have been taken away, and therefore the pure in heart are able to "see," as the angels behold, the face of God.

The name of the Lord on the foreheads of the Lord's servants signifies His ownership and protection. We belong to Christ. We have been baptized into Him and taken His name. We are His people. We will always be His people.

The promise of reigning with Christ calls Christians to trust in the Lord, to follow the Lamb, to remain faithful until the end. But whom will we reign over? Perhaps "to reign" means we will live as kings—satisfied and with every need met. We will live royally, in comfort and peace, secure and happy.

> *The angel said to me, "These words are trustworthy and true. The Lord, the God of the spirits of the prophets, sent his angel to show his servants the things that must soon take place" (22:6).*

The truth of Scripture is affirmed. The Word of God will stand forever. Even though the old heaven and earth have passed away, the Word of Jesus Christ is still trustworthy. And all that has been prophesied through John will take place soon.

"Soon"—the word will be repeated five times in Revelation 22, in verses 6, 7, 10, 12 and 20. Clearly, the message of Revelation is urgent. The Lord is expected ("A thousand years is like one day") soon. This is the hope of the Church.

The Lord Is Coming

> *"Behold, I am coming soon! Blessed is he who keeps the words of the prophecy in this book." I, John, am*

the one who heard and saw these things. And when I had heard and seen them, I fell down to worship at the feet of the angel who had been showing them to me. But he said to me, "Do not do it! I am a fellow servant with you and with your brothers the prophets and of all who keep the words of this book. Worship God!" (22:7-9).

Curtain down—the end of the world. Curtain up—the new heaven and new earth!

What the Church expects from the Lord: Come soon.

What the Lord expects from the Church: Keep the Word. Be faithful until the end. "Set your hope fully on the grace to be given you when Jesus Christ is revealed" (1 Pet.1:13).

Again John tries to worship God's messenger, and again he is stopped. The angel reminds John that he, John, and the prophets are all fellow servants, fellow messengers of God's Word.

Then he told me, "Do not seal up the words of the prophecy of this book, because the time is near. Let him who does wrong continue to do wrong; let him who is vile continue to be vile; let him who does right continue to do right; and let him who is holy continue to be holy" (22:10,11).

Sealing the book would mean closing it, shutting it up, hiding its message. But the angel affirms that the book of Revelation is not to be hidden. It is to be open, to be made known, to be read and understood (Rev. 1:3).

It is also a reminder that eternity will not offer

renewed opportunities of salvation. That which is holy and right will continue to be holy and right. That which is vile and wrong will remain so—and will be eternally shut off from all that is holy and right. There will be no bus from the fiery pit—no escaping hell, and no danger of losing heaven.

The call to repentance, then, is a call in the present. Repentance must not be put off into the future.

There comes a point in our lives when our direction is set, as in cement, by the many choices we have made. Once our course is determined, change becomes harder and harder, until finally it is impossible! In eternity, the righteous will be righteous and the evil will continue to be evil.

In this world—even at the end of our lives—we can always turn to Christ. In the next world, we will be unable to change; we will not even *desire* to change. The saints in heaven who reign with God certainly do not wish to leave. The inhabitants of hell will not prefer to be with the saints. Through our innumerable choices on earth, we take the road which leads upward or the road which ends below. That is the hard-core reality!

The judgment of the world pictured in Revelation illustrates the truth of hardening hearts. Most people choose not to repent, even when they believe God is bringing the judgment. They blaspheme the Lord but are unwilling to change the direction of their lives.

Therefore let the righteous continue in righteousness. Let those who are called to holiness be holy in their life *now*. Faithfulness will be rewarded with more than we can ever imagine: "No eye has seen, no ear has heard, no mind has conceived what God has prepared for those who love him" (1 Cor. 2:9).

As for the wicked, let them repent now. They are always called to repentance, as long as they are in the world (2 Pet. 3:9). While there is life, there is hope. Once they have reached their destination, there is no further possibility of change.

> *"Behold, I am coming soon! My reward is with me, and I will give to everyone according to what he has done. I am the Alpha and the Omega, the First and the Last, the Beginning and the End. Blessed are those who wash their robes, that they may have the right to the tree of life and may go through the gates into the city. Outside are the dogs, those who practice magic arts, the sexually immoral, the murderers, the idolaters and everyone who loves and practices falsehood" (22:12-15).*

When the Lord returns, He will reward the faithful. He is the sovereign Lord Who divides heaven and hell. He rewards the righteous and turns the wicked away. The wicked who are "outside" are not close to the city. They are not just outside its walls. "Outside" means shut out, away, not belonging to the kingdom of God.

Outsiders are without God. Insiders are with God.

Outsiders don't know. Insiders know.

Outsiders feel rejected. Insiders are accepted.

Those outside are called "dogs," originally a term for slaves. In the New Testament, "dogs" usually symbolizes unbelievers (see Matt. 7:6; Phil. 3:2).

Outsiders practice magic arts and do not trust in the sovereign Lord.

Outsiders worship other gods—materialism, hedonism, power, success and self.

Outsiders practice falsehood and are not faithful to the truth. They do not "walk in the truth" (3 John 3).

Insiders are faithful to the Lord. They have washed their robes in the blood of the Lamb. They show their faith by obedience. That is why they may enter through the gates into the city and eat of the tree of life.

Adam and Eve were kept from the tree of life after their fall. Because they wanted to be in charge, they were shut off from the Source of life. The tree of life is not for self-glory, but for the glory of God.

> "I, Jesus, have sent my angel to give you this testimony for the churches. I am the Root and the Offspring of David, and the bright Morning Star" (22:16).

Jesus is the One who gives the word.

Jesus is the root of David—that is, the Creator or Originator, the Lord of David.

Jesus is also the promised Messiah, the offspring of David, the One who fulfills the prophecies. He has earned the right to reign.

The bright morning star (see Rev. 2:28) is a symbol of world rule, authority, sovereignty. Jesus is the King of kings.

> The Spirit and the bride say, "Come!" And let him who hears say, "Come!" Whoever is thirsty, let him come; and whoever wishes, let him take the free gift of the water of life (22:17).

"We do not know what we ought to pray for, but the Spirit himself intercedes for us with groans that words cannot express" (Rom. 8:26). Here, the Holy Spirit prompts us to pray for the coming of our Lord. This is the expectation and hope of the bride, as she prepares for the wedding day, putting her faith into practice.

Here, in the final words of the book of Revelation, the invitation is extended once more to all the world: Come to the feast! The door is still open. Come and drink at the fountain. The water of life is free: "Without money and without cost" (Isa. 55:1). The mission of the Church is to preach the good news and prolong the offer of eternal life. The time is now.

A Final Warning

I warn everyone who hears the words of the prophecy of this book: If anyone adds anything to them, God will add to him the plagues described in this book. And if anyone takes words away from this book of prophecy, God will take away from him his share in the tree of life and in the holy city, which are described in this book (22:18,19).

The warning is explicit, and the consequences are serious. Eternal issues are at stake. No one is allowed to tamper with the Revelation! All interpreters and teachers (including myself) must pay attention. All readers must come with humility, devotion and openness of spirit. This is the inspired word of the living God!

Not only is this true for the book of Revelation. It holds for all of Scripture, for the Bible is "God-breathed" (2 Tim. 3:16).

Conclusion

He who testifies to these things says, "Yes, I am coming soon." Amen. Come, Lord Jesus (22:20).

One final time: "soon."

From the words of Jesus, we realize that the coming of Christ is next in the timetable of God. Nothing stands between us and that appearing.

But so much has happened since John first penned these lines. We are likely to wonder if these promises will be fulfilled. When? And why has it taken so long for Jesus to usher in the Kingdom?

We can find a direct answer in the book of 2 Peter, a reminder that God's timetable is not the same as ours: "With the Lord a day is like a thousand years, and a thousand years are like a day. The Lord is not slow in keeping his promise, as some understand slowness. He is patient with you, not wanting anyone to perish, but everyone to come to repentance" (3:8,9).

Nevertheless, Christians have always looked and longed for the coming of the Lord. And they have believed through the centuries that the day was not far off. Jesus Himself testified to the imminence of His coming. The early Christians lived by this promise. At the end of their worship service, they chanted, "Come, Lord Jesus." This became their regular closing as they met on the Lord's day.

During the course of Christian history, the urgency of that coming has faded, but it has never been rescinded!

Christians await the coming of the Lord. They pray for the swift consummation of history that will end the reign of sin and death and bring in the new heaven and the earth. Faith in the return of Christ is the fruit of faith in the risen Christ. Hope will not disappoint us (Rom. 5:5).

The book of Revelation ends with a similar benediction found in other books of the Bible:

> *The grace of the Lord Jesus be with God's people. Amen (22:21).*

This benediction emphasizes that the book of Revelation be read in the Christian fellowship—read and understood, read and practiced.

Revelation is the word of God for Christians!

Questions for Discussion and Meditation

1. What is new about the new heaven and earth?

2. What is the meaning of the holy city? Why is it described with such splendor?

3. How can we prepare for "the wedding?"

4. What is the last message of Jesus to the Church?

5. How are we to respond to that message?

Notes

Introduction

1. William Hendrickson, *More Than Conquerors* (Grand Rapids, MI: Baker, 1987).

Chapter 6

Revelation 8 and 9

1. E. F. Scott, *The Book of Revelation*, (London, 1939), quoted in Robert H. Mounce, *The Book of Revelation, New International Commentary* (Grand Rapids, MI: Eerdmans, 1977).

Chapter 10

Revelation 15 and 16

1. Note on Armaggeddon, *Scofield Reference Bible* (London: Oxford University Press, © 1917), pages 1348-1349.

2. Robert H. Mounce, *The Book of Revelation, New International Commentary* (Grand Rapids, MI: Eerdmans, 1977)., 302.

3. G. R. Beasley-Murray, *Revelation, New Century Bible Commentary* (Grand Rapids, MI: Eerdmans, 1987), 246.

Chapter 12

Revelation 19 and 20

1. Samuel J. Stone (1829–1900), "The Church's One Foundation." Public domain.

2. Sabine Baring-Gould (1834-1924), "Onward, Christian Soldiers." Public domain.

3. G. R. Beasley-Murray, *Revelation, New Century Bible Commentary* (Grand Rapids, MI: Eerdmans, 1987), 289.